TRUE LOVE STORIES FROM WORLD WAR TWO (WWII)

REAL LIFE LOVE STORIES OF COUPLES THROUGHOUT THE AGES

ROMANCE THROUGHOUT HISTORY

BOOK ONE

AMELIA KENTON

CONTENTS

To my husband, who's love inspired me to rekindle great love stories from the past.

INTRODUCTION

With every passing decade, we look back and realize that life has changed beyond measure. How we go about our daily routines, how we travel, even how we shop, these are all things which look nothing like they did twenty, thirty, or forty years ago.

The world changes at a fast pace, but within all that, our emotions remain the same.

To be human is to love. It doesn't matter if you're surrounded by technology or that you can do everything online without having to leave your sofa, or that you can travel the world with just a backpack. The bottom line is that we still have the same extreme and turbulent emotions as we did decades ago.

Perhaps, when you look at it that way, life doesn't change much at all.

Throughout history, some of the world's greatest love stories haven't only given us a window to the past, but they've shown us insights into what it takes to make love last. From fictional stories, such as Elizabeth Bennett and Mr. Darcy, to true life epics, we look at these romances and can't help but compare them to our own – for better or worse.

Of course, every love is different, and comparisons should never be taken too seriously, but there is always something to learn. After all, love isn't easy. Love is hard work.

Can you imagine what it might take to sustain a relationship during the hardest of times? During war, famine, or miles of distance? It might seem impossible, but throughout the centuries we've seen couples beat the odds and find their happily ever after. They never allowed petty misunderstandings or upsets to knock them off course and they never allowed their pride to get in the way either. Instead, they followed their hearts right to the end, wherever it led them.

That's what this book is about.

In a world of negativity and often cruelty, we all like to find solace in happily ever after. Throughout the darkest times of World War II, couples kept the roaring fires of passion alive in the most unlikely of ways. But back then, they didn't have Zoom calls or Facebook Messenger to give them an instant hit of feel-good vibes. They had to wait several weeks for a letter to land on their doormat, waiting desperately for the postman every single day and pushing down the dread of worry when a letter didn't arrive. It's not difficult to realize that during a world war, the post system probably isn't the most reliable either.

Can you imagine the sheer longing, fear, and heartbreak in living this way? A person you love is miles away, probably stationed and fighting on the front lines. Every day you worry that something may have happened to them and the longer it goes on without hearing from them, the more real your fears become. But then, one fateful day, your postbox makes that wonderful jangling sound, and an envelope falls onto your doormat.

The elation! That's a high that nothing can match.

The simplest of things have the power to make us the happiest, and what could be simpler than a letter. Stripping it back and focusing on the basics in life is something we've forgotten how to do. Everything is so complicated these days, and we often make it even harder through our actions, or our refusal to do anything at all.

But love is something worth fighting for, something worth risking it all for. It's also something many people have forgotten how to do.

Of course, pouring your heart out onto paper has never been simple. During World War II, there was very little option to do anything else; if you didn't tell your family and your lover how you felt, they would never know. Simply staying in touch through letters, albeit it irregular, meant that a connection could be kept. From there, a lifetime of love and affection could be developed – if fate gave you the chance.

But it took effort.

FIND INSPIRATION IN THE ENDURING LOVE OF OTHERS

This book isn't about looking at your relationship and realizing that you don't feel those sweeping highs from one side of the emotional spectrum to the other. Most people don't these days, and even back when love was billed as truly epic, couples still had dull days and misunderstandings. The truth is, there are many lessons to learn from the love stories of days gone by.

In these pages, you will find ten epic love stories that will take you from the edge of despair to the sheer indescribable feeling of elation. Some will move you to tears, others might make you laugh, and some might leave you wondering how you can start to improve your own relationships. It's very difficult not to become extremely invested in the characters and their heightened emotions when living through such desolate times as World War II. But then, these characters are all real.

Every couple we talk about lived their lives in the midst of war and bloodshed. Every single day brought new worry, fear, terror, bombs, gunfire, and death. But love has a habit of shining a bright light to help you navigate through hard times. In these cases, that's exactly what happened.

Of course, what you shouldn't expect from this book is a historically accurate recount of World War II. If you want to learn more about the ins and outs of the war, timelines, and milestones, perhaps you'll feel pushed to do more research as a result of the stories you read here. It's certainly something that's worthwhile, as history should always be remembered to ensure it never happens again. Learning about World War II will also help you to understand our couples better. But for now, we're focused on the intense and heart-wrenching love stories that took place against the background of world aggression.

Learn how relationships were sustained during the hardest of times and how even with miles of distance between them, constant worry, a very real chance of misunderstanding (we all know what the written word can be like), and the suppressed fear of their love never returning home, couples managed to endure. Even when it seemed like all hope had been lost, a tiny light kept things on course.

It's interesting to realize how relationships have changed over the years, and even though our lives are thankfully not the same as back then, that doesn't mean we can't learn lessons and use what we discover to improve our own relationships in the here and now. As you read each story, look for the small lessons you can learn and information you can take to try and create a deeper bond with your partner, or any partners you have in the future.

Real love takes work, perseverance, understanding, communication, and a whole lot of meeting each other halfway. Throw in a wartime situation and everything is heightened beyond measure. The longing, the fear, the never being able to dream of the future, and the loneliness. It's hard to imagine, but all of it is real and each of these couples made things work.

WHO AM I?

Before we go on, you might be wondering how I can sit here and tell you stories of couples who lived during the dark days of World War II. After all, I wasn't even alive back then.

The truth is, I've been fascinated with enduring love stories from the war for many years, and I've extensively researched all ten couples you're going to read about. They have captured my attention and my heart, and I hope they do the same for you. Their trials and tribulations, tears and heartbreaks created an endless pull on my heartstrings. I became so invested in their struggles, they took over my reality for a while.

After all, it's impossible not to feel a strong connection to a couple who's love letters you've read yourself. It's like sneaking a peek into someone's diary in many ways. You know you shouldn't look, but you can't quite help yourself.

The good news is that all the letters we're going to explore and talk about have been put into the public domain with the permission of the writers or their family members. In most cases, children and grandchildren of our World War II lovers wanted their stories to be told. They wanted future generations to understand the perseverance, refusal to give in, and sheer bravery their relatives showed.

The letters are inspirational and impossible to forget. That's what grabbed my attention and made me want to share these stories even further afield. I hope you find the same joy and interest as I did.

SETTLE DOWN FOR A SERIES OF LOVE STORIES LIKE NO OTHER

If you're someone who loves a good romance, you've come to the right place. These aren't your run-of-the-mill, chick-flick tales, and they're certainly not going to leave you dry-eyed either. In these pages, you'll find ten epic and nostalgic love stories told through the real-life letters sent from partner to partner, along with known background information about each person and their surroundings.

It's a precious peek into to the past and one that can help us understand that no matter the odds and no matter the distance, true love will always endure. Even in the darkest times, when no light can be found, hope seems futile, and the miles seem endless, love will find a way.

So, are you ready to be moved?

LOVE FROM AFAR - CHRISTOPHER AND BESSIE

Wartime London was a grim place. Certainly, during the war you could say that most places were, but in London, during the blitz, rationing, constant air-raid sirens, and black outs, most evenings life was a constant, dark cycle between work and sleep for most people. After all, what else was there to do?

Before the war, life was of course very different indeed. A thriving, bustling metropolis where men and women worked side by side and society was full of laughter and light. That light was quickly put out when war was declared on Nazi Germany. It was almost as if life changed literally overnight.

Prior to the war, Christopher Barker and Bessie Moore worked together at the local Post Office in their corner of London. At the time, Chris and Bessie were nothing more than co-workers who, although loose acquaintances, were never particularly close. Bessie had a boyfriend named Nick and Chris often chatted with him whenever he saw him out on the street. They never paid one another more attention than they should; such were the social norms of the time.

It was a pleasant and comfortable life for everyone, but when war was declared, many men were enlisted into the army and sent overseas to fight. Chris being one of them.

After signing up for national service, Chris was stationed in Libya, North Africa and worked as a signalman. Although he had his comrades beside him during his daily work, the constant fear and worry of an attack loomed large. He missed home and desperately wanted to see his family and friends. It seemed like time dragged and every second felt like a lifetime.

To pass the time, Chris started writing letters to everyone he knew back home, even those he didn't know all that well. One of those letters found its way to Bessie's doormat, addressed to her and her then boyfriend, Nick. However, little did Chris know that Nick and Bessie's relationship had ended, and she had managed to keep a clandestine secret all this time – that she had feelings for Chris when she was working with him at the Post Office, which possibly led to the downfall of her relationship with Nick. Bessie, like most women of the time, kept her feelings to herself and carried on with her life.

But faced with the uncertainty of war, Bessie wrestled with the idea of confessing her feelings once she received Chris's letter. In the end, she bravely decided to go for it. Bessie wrote a long letter back to Chris, asking how he was and using kind words in an attempt to cheer him up. Then she got to the crux of the matter – her relationship was over, and she could no longer deny her feelings for him. She was heartbroken that he was no longer working beside her and poured out her emotions in her first letter.

At that time, sending a letter wasn't a fast affair. There were no high-tech processes to zip snail mail from one side of the world to another, which meant Bessie had to wait a few weeks before she received a reply from her would-be lover. Every day she looked for the postman and was crestfallen when a reply didn't arrive.

But on the fateful day when a letter fell onto her mat, it sparked a back and forth correspondence that ended in both of them falling deeply in love. To this day, we have recovered around five hundred letters between the pair, full of words of longing, desperation, humor, and attempts to keep the others' spirits up and their connection real, even with all the miles and worry between them.

AN INNOCENT LOVE TOLD THROUGH LETTERS

When Christopher was posted to Libya, Bessie left her job at the Post Office and went to do her bit for the war effort. She began working as a Morse Code interpreter in London and soon after, her relationship with Nick deteriorated and ended. Nobody knows the exact reason for the breakdown of the relationship, but we can only assume that the stress of war took a toll. Perhaps Bessie's underlying feelings had something to do with it too! From her letters to Chris, we learn that she had bubbling feelings for a long time; confusing for her as she focused on her then-partner, Nick.

After receiving her first letter from Chris, innocently addressed to both her and Nick, Bessie knew that the only thing she could do was to tell the truth and confess her love. It wasn't easy for her. Confessing her feelings for a man who was stationed thousands of miles away would be considered crazy by most, but with the onset of war, perhaps Bessie, like many others, had gained the 'life is too short' mindset, and decided to open her heart bravely and innocently. What else could she do?

Of course, back in those days, women were not openly sexual and didn't speak of their feelings. However, in the letters between Chris and Bessie, we see Bessie becoming more and more frustrated at her inability to be with Chris intimately. In one letter she speaks of being glad that he has an extra blanket to keep him warm, but if she were there, he wouldn't need it. She admits to being a virgin and that she was desperate to be with him. Sick of waiting, she joked in one letter that she had "untapped resources" but then changed the subject to speak about mundane things such as pancakes!

On those long, dark nights, air-raid sirens echoing overhead, Bessie would sit and pen letters to her love. She didn't worry for her own safety, she poured all of her concern into her letters, urging Chris to be careful and to stay warm during the long, cold nights. She simply wanted him to come home to her safely so they could finally be together in every single way lovers should be.

Reflecting the wartime spirit, Bessie often referred to her fears and her loneliness, but then ended the sentence with the fact that everyone was in the same situation and that she knew it could always be worse. The 'glass half full' mindset helped Bessie keep her own spirits up and, unbeknownst to her, did the same for Chris. Bessie's constant positivity was a warming spirit to him, allowing him to focus on his future in her arms, rather than this present situation.

In every letter, Bessie's longing and loneliness was palpable. As Christmas came and went, she focused on the future, to the times when they could spend Christmases together and celebrate with family. At one point, she said she was so desperate to see him that she had considered going to the war office to sign up so she may be posted beside him or jumping in a boat and stowing away to Africa. Emotions bubbled up, heightened, and threatened to take her over. She knew she couldn't really do something so crazy, but her desire to be with Chris was so strong that at times, she would have done anything just for a second in his arms.

Those moments of intensity came and went, but Bessie's love never changed. It remained rock-solid, focused, intense, and always as deep as the ocean.

A MAN'S LOVE HELD BACK THROUGH FEAR

The interesting thing about reading Chris and Bessie's letters is the difference between the two in terms of how they communicated. Perhaps it's stereotypical to say, but Bessie's prose is emotional, open, joking sometimes, before letting down her guard and pouring her entire heart out onto paper. Desperate with fear and longing, she couldn't hide her emotions even if she tried. For sure, Bessie was a 'what you see, is what you get' kind of a woman.

On the other hand, Chris tried his best to hold back how he felt, although most of the time quite unsuccessfully. His love for Bessie knew no bounds and seeped through his words no matter how hard he tried. Although initially surprised that she had written back to him and confessed her feelings for him, letters between the two had allowed them to get to know each other on a deeper level, and love soon crept in.

For Chris, Bessie's letters kept him going. His spirits soared higher than the clouds themselves whenever he received a reply from her, and soon enough, he started dreaming of their future together once the war was over. However, he worried about what people would say and what their friends and family would think about their budding love, especially as Bessie had been in a relationship when they were working together originally. Would people think they had been seeing each other behind her then-partner's back? It would have been such a scandal, even with a war going on.

Remember, back in those days, it was very easy to cause drama and people loved to talk. For sure, it still happens nowadays but we don't care as much as we did back then. Something as simple as a man being seen out on the street with a woman he wasn't acquainted with could cause tongues to wag. The woman could be disgraced, and the man talked about negatively as a 'cad' for months afterward.

So understandably, Chris was a little concerned about their future together after the war, yet he didn't allow it to stop them dreaming and he was carefully making plans on how to navigate any potential issues. In one particular letter, he jokingly enquired about whether she was Roman Catholic or not, because that would have caused a stir amongst his family and perhaps posed a few problems they would need to somehow overcome as a couple.

In many of Chris' letters, it's easy to tell that his mind was busy flitting from one moment to the next. Idle in his thoughts other than the fear of his posting in Libya, he often said things like, "I hope you won't mind that I need to see my family first," and "please don't tell too many people right now, I'm worried that it won't work out well." Very aware of causing a social stir, Chris was meticulously planning their future, even when nobody knew whether the future would come or not.

Perhaps this was Chris' way of getting through the daily grind. Terrified in his life, scared every day that something would happen to him, he projected that onto Bessie in the most caring of ways; telling her to be careful when she crossed the road in London and to make sure she stayed safe for him when he returned home. Even though he was facing extreme danger every second of the day, he was more focused on her navigating London's streets in safety.

In one notable letter, joy permeated Chris' prose and you could easily see what Bessie meant to him. He had been given news that he would be returning home to England for leave. He could hardly contain himself. Jumping from subject to subject, plan to plan, and back to worry, Chris told Bessie to wait for a telegram to announce his return and another when he was on his way to England. He would have to see his parents first, but he was desperate to be with her. "The most important thing is just to be with you."

A HAPPILY EVER AFTER

After years of back-and-forth correspondence, the fateful day finally came – Chris returned and ran into Bessie's arms. Can you imagine? All that longing, all that desperation, all that worry, all flooding out in that one second of elation and joy?

Years of talking, banter, compromise, darkness, and loneliness. Through all of that, this couple developed a close friendship, a deep love, and managed to hold onto it all no matter what life threw at them. Could it happen today? You have to wonder.

Once the war ended, the couple married, and they went on to have a son together. After Chris died, their son, Bernard, was sorting through some old belongings and remembered the small, blue box that his father had given to him just before he died. Keen to learn its contents, Bernard opened the box and 500 rolled up letters fell into his lap.

Those letters took Chris and Bessie's son on a whistlestop tour of their enduring and deep love. Five hundred letters of blue paper, crumbled and creased with years, clear handwriting scrawled across the pages – talk about a true window to the past and what a wonderful keepsake for Bernard, documenting his parents deep and lasting love for one another. There truly is no better gift.

Most of the letters Chris wrote to Bessie were kept, but most of the letters that Bessie wrote to Chris had been destroyed to keep them out of prying eyes. Always careful of someone getting the wrong idea, Chris wanted to protect Bessie as much as possible. But you can certainly imagine that her words were imprinted in his memory.

The letters between Chris and Bessie show us the danger of Chris' life as a conscript in North Africa, Greece, and Italy. As he moved around, Bessie's fears grew and although Chris never really went into much detail to tell her about his daily life, out of concern for her, she knew that it was a lot worse than he was describing.

Within all of this, we can understand the boredom, tedium, and endless amount of waiting Chris endured in between times of combat.

For Bessie, she simply wanted her man to return home so she could begin a passionate love affair that, in her mind, had no end date. Chris was desperate to travel back to England and jump into Bessie's arms, although always mindful of what people may say about their new love. In the end, none of it mattered as the couple married and went on to live a happy life together.

We can learn a lot from Bessie and Chris. How many people these days are that patient? How many people are that dedicated and faithful? How many are that vulnerable and open? They didn't only make it to their happily ever after, they survived every storm thrown at them. They were prepared to lay their hearts on the line for love, even though every letter took weeks to be received and even longer to receive a reply. None of it mattered because they loved each other.

Bessie and Chris' love letters have been published since their son found them, keen to show the world his parents' enduring love. Actor Benedict Cumberbatch even read some of the letters aloud on stage, playing the part of Chris. Their words have captured the world's attention and shown everyone what true love really looks like.

Even in death, you can imagine that Bessie and Chris are still together, entwined forever, and safe in the knowledge that no matter what happens now, they're back home where they belong – together.

2

MY DEAREST BELOVED DIANA –
LENNY & DIANA MILLER

L ife has a habit of changing on a dime. One minute everything seems wonderful, filled with joy and hope for the future, but then, a cataclysmic event happens and the world is turned upside down.

For most people during World War II, that's exactly how life was.

Hope and happiness were replaced by fear and worry. Bright days suddenly became dull, and lonely nights seemed to go on forever.

Bustling Brooklyn, New York, was a vibrant place to live prior to December 7, 1941. Just as it is today, you'd see people running from place to place, music on street corners, laughter, and a lot of conversation. But, after the Japanese bombing of Pearl Harbor, everything changed.

When the USA declared war on Japan, the country threw itself into World War II, forcing millions of men between the ages of eighteen to forty-five to be drafted overseas to join the war effort. This was the moment when millions of couples found themselves separated and facing thousands of miles between them, unsure if they would ever see each other again.

Can you imagine the terror, fear, and uncertainty? Life was put on pause, and nobody knew for how long.

For Lenny and Diana Miller, a young, married couple from Brooklyn, life had been idyllic. They were both in the first flourishes of married life, enjoying their honeymoon period, and bursting with delight when they found out Diana was pregnant with their first child. Everything was going exactly as they had planned, and they couldn't have wished for more.

Yet, everything was about to turn on that dime we mentioned earlier.

STANDING UP TO FASCISM WITH A DEEP, ENDURING LOVE

Lenny and Diana were both children of Jewish immigrants who had fled Eastern Europe. As such, they had a deep understanding of their roots and were actively involved in local labor groups. Both were well-educated, eager-readers, and always keen to learn more. The events in Europe had caused them deep concern and, although they followed the news, they had hoped that the war wouldn't extend to their shores. If it did, they weren't sure how that would affect their relationship, their families, or their friends. It caused them extreme worry, but they tried to focus on their future.

Having heard stories from their parents, both Lenny and Diana had a deep and enduring hatred of any form of fascism. But that's exactly what Nazi Germany stood for. For millions of Jews in Europe, it wasn't only their dreams that were being shattered, but their lives being taken from them. All of this filled both Lenny and Diana with extreme sorrow, and they knew that no matter how hard it might be, they couldn't just sit by and watch.

When the draft was announced, Lenny decided to head down

to the local office and put his name down. Of course, he was terrified and questioned a million times whether he was doing the right thing, but what else could he do? If he didn't do his duty, he would be betraying every relative in his bloodline, while simultaneously letting down his country. Despite her deep fear of what may happen, Diana supported her husband's decision. With their unborn child growing every day, Diana put on a brave face and did what she'd done all her life – face whatever may come next.

For Lenny, being separated from his young wife and unborn child was heartbreaking. He questioned the decision in his mind several times over but knew that he had to do the right thing. If he didn't fight for the lives of those who couldn't, who else would? He simply wasn't the type of man to turn his back and ignore the pain and suffering of others. He could only hope that in the end, it would all be worth it.

Lenny was an intelligent man and spoke English, German, French, and Yiddish. Despite his qualifications offering him a higher position, and perhaps a safer one in some ways, Lenny wanted to be enlisted as a private and serve his time as a rifleman. At first, Diana was understandably aghast at his decision; that was the most dangerous type of posting! How could her husband put himself in such danger when their unborn child needed him?

Yet, Diana and Lenny were cut from the same cloth. Despite her completely understandable reservations, Diana gave him her blessing. Terrified and wracked with worry about their future, she took a deep breath, pulled back her shoulders, and held her head high. She had faith in Lenny, he was that kind of guy.

As Lenny departed for basic training, Diana continued to work in a factory making submarine periscopes. She knew this work probably wouldn't last for long, as her growing belly meant that soon she would have a child to look after all on her own. However, she did what she could and saved any money she could get her hands on. She knew she would need it when the baby came and for however long Lenny was gone.

Whenever Diana allowed herself to think too much, her mind would drift to scenarios of Lenny never returning home, never meeting their child, and of her spending her days alone. But Diana was a strong woman, and whenever these thoughts came, she forced herself to push them away and get back down to business. She couldn't allow the darkness to swallow her up, she had a child to think about, and she wouldn't allow the fascism and prejudices of those who had started this wretched war affect their child's attitudes and life.

This type of strength in the face of extreme hardship is rare these days. Back then, women were strong because they had no choice. If they allowed themselves to dwell or think too much, the terror would take them over and drag them down. Diana knew she had to fight for her unborn child and keep her spirits up for Lenny. There was no other option.

The best way to do that, she decided, was to start keeping her husband up to date with life via letters. That way, they maintained their connection, Lenny knew what was happening back home, and she could help to keep his spirits up. It was their type of normalcy in very abnormal times.

PUTTING PEN TO PAPER

As with most wartime couples, letters were the only way to stay in touch and even delivery of those letters took weeks. Sometimes letters never came because they were lost in transit. Patience was certainly needed during those times, but when your heart is thousands of miles away and you're full of fear and anxiety, it's extremely difficult to keep a clear head. Add to that pregnancy hormones, and Diana often felt she was losing her mind.

Sometimes the waiting took its toll on Diana, so to try and keep her mind busy, she organized a worker's union in the factory. The group would come together for regular meetings and discuss events overseas, such as Italy's surrender or the Red Army's march forward.

Diana kept Lenny up to date with her group's discussions and he was full of pride. Here was his wife, almost full-term, about to give birth, and still as focused on social activism as ever before. Lenny knew that if his wife could be this strong, so could he, and it gave him the push to keep going.

Between 1943 and 1946, Lenny and Diana wrote more than 2500 letters to each other. Of course, this isn't unusual for wartime couples, but the sheer number is eye opening! They wrote to each other every single day as Lenny and Diana knew the only way to stay connected and to keep their heads up was to share their thoughts and feelings. For them, it was almost like a running dialogue or conversation, as if they were in the same room.

In one particular letter, Lenny speaks of his hopes for the future and life after the army. "And we will endure that too, and go on loving and fighting, 'til the day we can lay my uniform aside in the mothballs." Despite his commitment to his job and the service he knew he had to provide, Lenny was keen to live a normal life. He knew that life would still have its challenges after that time, but the tough time they'd been through during the war would stand them in good stead no matter what came their way.

Sometimes their letters would become full of emotion, other times they would be a series of events. It didn't matter what the content was, it was the connection over the miles that mattered. Lenny always addressed his letters, "My dearest, beloved Diana ..." and unlike most soldiers, he managed to save every single letter he received from his wife.

In most cases, letters would be lost because soldiers simply didn't have anywhere to store them. But Lenny wasn't like most soldiers, and he came up with a unique way to save every word his beloved wife sent him. By storing her letters in his gas mask, reading them and absorbing every last bit of emotion from them, and then mailing them back to her so she could keep them safe, all his letters were kept. He dreamed of them sitting together once the war was over, reading them, and remembering everything they had gone through. Their dream of making it out the other side of this nightmare kept them both going through the long, dark nights and hardships to come.

And there were hardships. Many of them. Yet, throughout their struggles, they had a mantra they repeated to one another constantly: "we are going to be lucky."

A YOUNG MOTHER'S STRUGGLE

As their unborn child grew and the due date came closer and closer, Diana began to worry about how they would survive without money. She couldn't work in the factory and look after a baby while also being plagued with worries about how she would manage as a first-time mother.

When Diana finally gave birth to their daughter, Elizabeth, she sent a letter to Lenny to tell him every last detail about her. She explained as much as she could about the birth (men didn't really want to know about those things back then) and described their daughter's tiny features and how she looked like the both of them. The emotion in her words dripped onto the page and she hoped that Lenny would feel the pride and love she felt for their new baby daughter.

Just looking at Elizabeth gave Diana the strength to carry on. For Lenny, waiting to hear news of his daughter's birth was excruciating and, due to the slow pace of the worldwide post system at that time, he didn't get to hear that he had become a father until ten days after the event. But that didn't stop him from bursting with pride and joy at the news. Even though everything around him was dark and desperate, Elizabeth's arrival had brought technicolor light back to his life.

Throughout the long, sleepless nights that parenthood brings, Diana would sometimes allow herself to think about how things should have been. Lenny would have been beside her; they would have taken it in turns to soothe Elizabeth as she cried, following every step of their daughter's first few months of life with joy, soaking it all up like a sponge. Perhaps they would have documented her milestones, from her first tooth, her first words, and her first steps, in photographs or words.

But those dreams had been shattered. Instead, Lenny was facing terror every day on the frontlines, never knowing if he would make it to the end of the day alive. Diana was home, worrying about how they would pay for food, trying to soothe their baby daughter, and wishing that she had her husband with her. Whenever the dark worry of whether she would ever see her husband again rose, she desperately pushed it back down, breathing through it and focusing on Elizabeth.

Diana was lonely, lost, and yearning for Lenny with every single second that passed. But she never quite let him know just how lonely she was. Her letters were as upbeat as she could muster the strength to be. She mostly talked about life and how she was trying to find another job so she could earn some money while taking care of Elizabeth. She tried to keep Lenny's spirits up by talking about the days they would spend together when he returned home and describing every small step in Elizabeth's progress.

None of this was easy, of course, and when Diana didn't hear word from Lenny for 46 days, she began to fear the worst. Where was he? Was he alive? Was he dead?

Lenny had been sent to the frontlines in France and he had no opportunity to write or send a letter home. He knew Diana would be terribly worried but there was simply nothing he could do. Yet the moment he could send word of his arrival in France and that he was okay, he did so. The sheer burst of joy when that envelope dropped on the mat was as though every wrong in the world had been righted once more.

But coming from a family of Jewish immigrants, both Lenny and Diana knew that wrongs were not being righted, and if anything, they were getting worse with every passing day. Prior to the war, the couple had always shared their deep passion for social justice, but they never dreamed they would be out there fighting it quite so directly.

Yet somehow, it didn't feel that heroic.

FIGHTING FOR HIS LIFE

Lenny had never been a man to shy away from his duties, but even his strength and fortitude was tested during his time in combat. A man who was focused on doing good, he sometimes allowed his mind to wander to the 'what if' part of the equation. What if the war had never happened? What if he had taken a so-called easier posting? What would their life be like at home?

Shattered hopes and dreams were a common theme for couples all around the world during World War II. Everyone had a dream, a plan, and hope for the future, and they all came to an abrupt pause. Lenny often wondered whether they would be un-paused or whether they had come to a definite full stop.

In July 1944, Lenny was fighting in France and was assigned to the intelligence section of a battalion. As always, he threw himself into the posting and tried to keep his mind off the constant gnawing of fear and worry. He thought of Diana and Elizabeth every single second of the day. Diana's letters kept him up to date with his growing daughter, but he longed to see her for himself. He wanted to touch her hair, inhale her unique scent, and hold her for the first time.

Lenny knew that Diana was interested in what was happening

on the frontlines, but he couldn't tell her too much. Confidentiality was key to avoid secrets reaching enemy hands, but he tried his best to describe everything as briefly as he could. Diana was an intelligent woman, and he knew that leaving out small details would cause her to put the pieces together and perhaps come to the wrong conclusion.

However, despite his efforts, Lenny underestimated just how strong Diana was in the face of such hardship. Her fortitude is evident in her letters. She was terrified, of course she was, but she focused on the positives, even when they were so difficult to find. Identifying a silver lining in such situations may seem impossible to many, but Diana wasn't like most women.

Not wanting to keep too many details from Diana, but also not wanting to make her worry unnecessarily, Lenny was as open as possible about events in his life. He shared that he had been injured in artillery fire and survived a bombing. He also explained how he received a Silver Star for heroism during the Battle of the Bulge. Despite wishing that her husband wasn't in such situations, Diana was bursting with pride.

Her husband, a hero!

But their letters back and forth also tell of anguish and gut-wrenching fear. Even the strongest couples are tested in such situations. On one occasion, Lenny was hospitalized after becoming wounded in battle. Diana didn't know the true extent of his injuries, but Lenny was desperate to send a letter to her and explain before she received a call from the War Office telling her about it.

Even during pain, terror, fear, and worry, Lenny was only ever thinking about Diana. It was all he could do to get through each day.

The bond they shared was unbreakable, deep as the ocean, and it was exactly what Lenny needed to push him through the darkness. The echoes of gunfire in the air, the stench of death all around, a constant churning gut, and being so cold he couldn't feel his extremities, all of this was made easier because there was a bright light waiting for him at home.

AND THEN IT WAS ALL OVER

When something has come into your life and bulldozed everything you've ever known, it's a strange feeling when you wake up one morning and it's all over. It's like the darkness has lifted and suddenly you can see a bright light in the sky – is that the sun?

Did it all really happen or was it a nightmare?

When the war ended, both Lenny and Diana didn't know quite what to do. Was it really over? Dare they dream again? Both were terrified that if they started to open up that small window of hope again, another crushing disappointment would rain down on them. But no, this time it was real.

Reunited, they had beaten all the odds. Their shattered dreams could finally be pieced back together again, as they'd made it. A couple with a Jewish background had beaten the odds, survived, and not only that, but they'd also come out of it stronger than they went into it. They were parents now, desperate to let their child know just how strong their love was. After all, a child raised in this type of deep, enduring love, would never know any pain.

And endure she did. Elizabeth L. Fox, the couple's daughter, came across her parent's letters and was absorbed from the first one. What a love story! How brave they were! She knew that the world simply had to read this story.

To this aim, Elizabeth, put the sections of the letters together into a book, and aptly named it, "We Are Going to be Lucky."

Through three years of extreme struggles, uncertainty, distance, fear, anguish, and terror, Lenny and Diana weren't lucky. After all, lucky is something simply bestowed upon you for the sake of it. Lenny and Diana earned their luck. Through writing a letter to one another every single day, pushing aside the sickening fear that they would never see one another again, and forcing themselves to see the light in the darkness, this is a love story that goes beyond the regular.

Lenny and Diana's deep respect for social justice and hatred of fascism pushed them into action. Lenny knew he couldn't just stand aside and do nothing, and Diana knew that she couldn't stop her husband from doing his duty. Nor would she ever ask him to. They put their faith in a higher power and focused on their love. Because at the end of the day, if love can't pull you through, what else can?

So many people these days focus on the easy option. It would have been easy for Lenny to accept a safer posting; it would have been easy for Diana to give in to her fear and spend her days in constant despair. But neither allowed it. They did what they had to do, and, in the end, they were rewarded with being reunited, a life-long love that, even as the years pass by, will never die.

3

FORBIDDEN LOVE – FELICE & LILLY

You can't choose who you fall in love with. Love comes along out of the blue, sweeps you up, and takes you on a journey that you're almost powerless to stop. For some couples during World War II, their love stories weren't only tested by distance and worry of never seeing each other again, but by other elements that were equally out of their control.

Our next story is a little different from the previous ones. There is only a small amount of distance here, but a whole lot of trouble that threatened to tear our lovers apart. Facing battles every single day became exhausting, but they never allowed themselves to close their eyes to the threats around them.

The 1940s were a relatively conservative time. It wasn't hard to cause a scandal; simply walking down the street with a little more flesh showing than normal would have people whispering and curtains twitching. But same sex relationships? These were definitely talked about in hush tones.

Lilly Wust and Felice Schragneheim were meant to be, and nothing could stand in their way. Bigotry, discrimination and Hitler all tried their luck pulling them apart, but their love was destined to endure.

However, the start wasn't quite so rosy.

LILLY'S REGULAR "LOVE" STORY

For Lilly, life was relatively calm. Born to a traditional family in Berlin in 1913, as Charlotte Kappler, she grew up in the midst of World War I, but kept her head down and away from politics. Lilly preferred to focus on fun and creativity, staying away from the darkness and dread that war always brings.

However, her carefree life turned on its head when she celebrated her 20th birthday. At this time, Adolf Hitler had just been elected as the Chancellor of Germany and nobody had any clue what was about to come next. Of course, Hitler's election success was slowly stirring up his Nazi sympathizers, rallying them to the so-called "cause" he pushed forward.

In the midst of all the political fervor, Lilly was focused on matters of the heart. As was often the case in those days, Lilly married young. She fell in love with a banking accountant named Gunther Wust and, as she was swept away by the passionate stirrings of first love, she didn't wait to tie the knot. Her parents were less than pleased. Gunther had clear Nazi sympathies and, as followers of the former communist party, Lilly's parents were distrusting of the new regime and everything it stood for.

But Lilly? Well, Lilly didn't want to listen to her parents. A headstrong, passionate woman, she threw herself into her new role as housewife to her beloved Gunther. She was soon pregnant with their first child, with several more to follow afterward.

Despite the children, wartime stress took a toll on the young couple, and before long, Gunther's wandering eye started shift. Several extramarital affairs happened on both sides, as Lilly's desperation for love and affection took her away from her martial bed as well. To her shock, one of those affairs resulted in her falling pregnant with another boy, her fourth child.

Little did Lilly know it at the time, but her unfortunate pregnancy would turn out to be a blessing in disguise. At the time, any mother giving birth to boys was seen as giving birth for Hitler. This new baby meant she was now eligible for the 'Mother Cross,' an award that bestowed many advantages upon Lilly's household, including a housemaid.

The arrival of that housemaid would change everything.

A DESTINED CONNECTION

Inge Wolf applied for the housemaid position in the Wust household. She was duty-bound to do her year of domestic service, but nobody knew that during her down time, she was a German supporter of the Jews, fighting underground for their freedom from repression and violence.

As you can imagine, such leanings were severely frowned upon in Nazi Germany. Anyone caught assisting Jews was threatened with jail or worse. But love has a way of finding its destined pair and Inge would turn out to be the helping hand along the way.

Many Jews fled Germany and hid far away from Hitler's political machine, but many stayed in the country and hid in plain sight, usually in the households of those who had earned the Mother Cross. This is how Felice Schragenheim met Lilly Wust.

Lilly had taken her housemaid, Inge, out for a coffee in central Berlin and Inge had invited her friend Felice along. That moment. Those sparks. Lilly would never forget it. The moment they locked eyes, it was like passion was burning through the short distance between them. She found it amazing that nobody could tell!

Lilly was confused about the feelings she was experiencing for the passionate, dark-haired woman she'd just met. Felice was eight years younger than Lilly and told her that she was the daughter of a dentist. She gave few other details about her identity, scared to open up and admit that she was Jewish.

But Felice had many problems and not telling Lilly her true identity was only one of them. Her family had all been deported and, despite having received her own deportation notice, Felice refused to leave. She chose to go into hiding instead – always the passionate risk-taker.

It was this desire for change that drove Felice to take a job at a Nazi newspaper. You might wonder why an ardent Jew would want to work in such a place, but she saw it as her duty to try and extract information from the inside and help others in her situation. Just like Inge, Felice worked in the underground, helping Jews flee and hide.

As Felice sat and spoke to Lilly, with Inge looking on, she became more and more curious about this seemingly normal housewife. Felice could tell that there was a fire burning inside of Lilly, and she was far from the ordinary Nazi wife. She was keen to find out more.

Being in such close proximity to the perceived enemy thrilled Felice and called out to her risk-taking tendencies. She wanted to see how far she could push this situation, so she began visiting Inge at the house and staying as long as she could. Gunther was never around, but when he was, he could tell that Lilly seemed happier and full of energy. This pleased him, as he had long noticed his wife becoming withdrawn and lethargic.

If only he had known the reason for her renewed passion for life.

Lilly and Felice began swapping letters, poems, compliments, and even bought one another flowers. Their friendship was slowly ebbing away and being replaced by something altogether more clandestine.

ABSENCE MAKES THE HEART GROW FONDER

The situation in Nazi Germany worsened for the Jews and Felice was eventually forced to flee to avoid being detected. Berlin was no longer safe for her, and she sought solace with friends in the mountains. Of course, Lilly couldn't understand where Felice had gone or why she left. She mistakenly thought that she had done something wrong, and she became lost and withdrawn in her absence.

The days seemed to drag on for Lilly. She was back to having no distraction from her doomed love affair with Gunther, who was forced to spend more and more time away from home due to work and his personal sympathies toward Hitler. But one fateful day, Lilly's mood went from dark to jubilant. A letter fell onto her doormat, and she instantly recognized the handwriting.

At the time, she tried her best not to analyze these feelings too much. She knew that falling in love with another woman would bring a world of shame to her parents, but she also knew that she was at a loss to stop the maelstrom of feelings she was experiencing. Preferring to push the 'whys and wherefores' aside, she ripped open the letter and read with greedy anticipation.

This letter wasn't the first and over the course of the coming weeks, Felice's letters made Lilly feel a sense of love and contentment that she'd never felt with Gunther. She suddenly felt alive, connected in a way that she'd never done before, and although she was still yet to learn the truth about her would-be lover, life felt light and full of energy once more.

Of course, we know that every great love story never goes quite so smoothly, and that was certainly the case for Lilly. She was soon admitted to hospital with a serious infection and stayed there for several weeks. Felice became wracked with worry and despite the danger of leaving her safety net in the mountains, she rushed back to Berlin to be by Lilly's side.

It was as though Felice's presence worked better than any antibiotic ever could, and Lilly's condition slowly but surely improved. As Felice arrived at her bedside, the couple shared their first tender kiss, a date marked clearly in Lilly's diary.

TROUBLE ON THE HORIZON

The couple's relationship moved quickly after that first tender kiss in the hospital. Once Lilly was discharged back home, they had a secret wedding ceremony and reveled in their close yet clandestine connection. It was as though they had a deep secret from the world, something that nobody could damage or pull apart; as long as only they knew, nobody could ruin it or tarnish the beauty of their love.

Lilly and Felice were a couple like no other and were keen to avoid following the norm. To celebrate their love for one another, the couple wrote their own wedding vows, something that was quite rare at that time. Felice decided to create a list of ten promises to Lilly, combining her deep love and her promises of daily life.

1. I will always love you
2. I will never leave you
3. I will do everything I can to make you happy
4. I will provide for you and the children as much as conditions allow
5. I won't object to you providing for me
6. I won't look at pretty girls anymore, at most to confirm that you're prettier
7. I won't come home late very often
8. I will try to grind my teeth quietly at night
9. I will always love you
10. I will always love you .... until further notice

At this time, Gunther was moved to a frontline position and Felice moved into the family home as Lilly's caretaker. The war was getting worse by the day and more and more Jews were facing extreme persecution. Felice's mood darkened as more news filtered through from the underground, yet she was terrified of opening up and telling her new wife the truth about her identity.

What if she turned her in? Or worse, in Felice's mind, what if she was disgusted and pushed her away?

To keep them both safe, Felice often disappeared at a moment's notice and Lilly began to feel insecure and suspicious about her whereabouts. Had she found someone else? During one passionate argument, Lilly threatened to leave and at that moment, the dam broke.

Felice's true identity poured from her like a roaring stream. She held nothing back. She was desperate to keep Lilly, even if it meant risking her life. She admitted she was Jewish and that she was running to save her own life.

Despite Felice's fears, Lilly didn't turn her nose up in disgust or call the Gestapo. Instead, she soaked up Felice's story with all the passion she'd received and allowed the experience to bring them closer. Nobody would take Felice away from her, Lilly decided.

Felice felt a huge sense of relief at finally telling Lilly her true identity, but she still kept many details of her underground activities to herself. She was determined to keep Lilly and her children safe and didn't want to incriminate her in any way. Felice's friends in the underground were less than impressed with their comrade's confession and worried that Lilly would report them all for their activities.

They needn't have worried. Lilly's desperate love for Felice protected every single one of them.

FREEDOM, BUT FOR HOW LONG?

Gunther's Nazi sympathies ultimately caught up with him as he died during a mission on the Eastern Front. Lilly's divorce came through in 1943 and the new couple were free to live their lives, without any worry of Lilly's husband getting in the way.

The next 18 months were blissful for the couple, despite the fighting, persecution, and worry that clouded every day. They refused to allow outside influences to ruin their love for one another, and shared wonderful experiences, from long walks together, to simple things like making dinner at home.

Yet, war always ebbs and flows, and life became even more dangerous than ever before for underground Jews in Berlin. Felice and her friends were being watched and every single day was shrouded in danger and worry. They were no longer safe and had to escape.

But Felice? Felice was a risk-taker, and she was in love. Did this make her vulnerable? Perhaps so.

The reason for her decision to stay isn't documented in her diary, but you don't really need words to understand why. She loved Lilly and she wouldn't leave her side, no matter how dangerous the situation. She would rather face the risk of being sent away than leave the woman she loved with her whole heart.

Her decision seemed to be a safe one for a short while. They carried on as best they could, despite the looming fear that clouded every day.

On a surprisingly bright August day in 1944, the couple had gone out for a walk. Carefree and enjoying one another's company, they were giggling and linking arms. Then they walked into their apartment.

The Gestapo were waiting, ready to arrest Felice. Lilly was also arrested but after interrogation, she was released without charge. In Lilly's mind, she would have preferred to have been taken away herself. Life without Felice by her side felt unbearable and she couldn't stand to think of a second without her beloved with her.

From that moment on, the couple never saw one another again. Lilly felt like someone had turned off the lights and she was plunged into darkness.

FIGHTING FOR HER LOVE'S LEGACY

This story is probably unique in specific details, but when you delve deeper, you're sure to find many other couples who were pulled apart by the simple fact that one was Jewish and the other wasn't. Nazi Germany was obviously the single worst place in the world to be a Jew, but most didn't want to hide; they did what they had to do to survive, but poured their attention into fighting for freedom in the underground, just as Felice had done.

In September 1944, Felice was sent to Auschwitz and after that, she was transferred to the Gross-Rosen concentration camp. Once the camp was evacuated, prisoners were sent on death marches to other camps, and it's thought that Felice either died on the journey or at the next camp.

Lilly never knew the final resting place of her beloved. She never got to say goodbye, kiss her one last time, or tell her that she loved her. Yet Felice knew all of this already. It was evident in the way Lilly looked her, held her hand, and stood by her side even when she knew she was putting herself in grave danger. None of it mattered. All that mattered was love.

Lilly Wust lived to the grand old age of 92 years, but she made sure she made the very most of those years without Felice by her side.

Desperate to pull some kind of silver lining out of a terrible and heart-breaking situation, Lilly poured all her efforts into helping other Jewish women like Felice. She never wanted to see another woman suffer the same horrific fate as Felice, simply for being who they were.

For her efforts, Lilly was awarded the German Federal Service Cross in 1981 and she achieved one of Israel's most prestigious honors – The Righteous Among The Nations.

Of course, Lilly would have passed all of this to one side if she could have lived out her old age with Felice by her side. She often dreamed of her lost love, wondering about the 'what ifs' and 'maybes'. What if they'd met at a different time? What if they'd fled sooner?

But Lilly was pragmatic. She knew that no amount of wondering could ever bring back her one true love, so she did her best to honor her memory in the only way she knew how – by fighting for justice. It's what Felice would have wanted.

Bigotry, hate, and cruelty have no place in the world, but we don't live in an ideal world either. During World War II, neither sense nor reason held any place in society. A sheer unexplained hatred of Jews saw families, marriages, friendships, and relationships ripped apart at the seams. The sheer number of broken hearts and lost legacies is astounding and heartbreaking.

Lilly and Felice might be a story of polar opposites, but they are a clear example of how love really can conquer all.

4

A NAVY LOVE STORY – GILBERT &
ELEANOR

A declaration of a war is always a shock, no matter how many people saw it coming. Political tensions may cause people to be nervous and worry about the possible outcome, but nobody ever wishes for war. We consider the possibility but push it back down as quickly as it arises. After all, thinking about it too much is terrifying.

But World War II, as with most wars, was inevitable. Countries couldn't sit around and watch Hitler's persecution and terror sweep across Europe and beyond. And when other countries joined forces with Nazi Germany, a real threat to civilization as we knew formed.

When the USA joined the war after the attack on Pearl Harbor by the Japanese, everyone worried. The violence and terror of the Pearl Harbor attack had opened people's eyes to a new way to fight – a method that included the potential for nuclear armory, weapons like no other and violence that had no place in the world. The world had to answer.

The drafting of soldiers meant anyone eligible for service was duty-bound to do their part for the war effort, no matter what their jobs or qualifications were before. While many would rather have ignored the call or perhaps hidden or run, most knew that they would be shamed by those around them if they didn't answer positively. It was a man's duty to do his part, and a woman's duty to do all she could back home.

Can you imagine how hard it must have been to get up and decide to go to the drafting office to put your name forward? In the knowledge that you would be sent to another country to fight and may never return home to see your loved ones?

That was the reality for many.

DOING HIS DUTY

For Gilbert Steingart, his years of studying dentistry had helped him build up a strong and successful private practice. He had a loving wife named Eleanor and two beloved daughters whom he doted upon. Yet, when war was declared via a crackly TV and radio announcement, he knew he had to put down his white dentist's coat and do what every man was duty-bound to do.

Of course, he questioned his actions for a second. His life at home had been charming to a degree. He didn't want to give any of that up, but then he thought of the soldiers being killed daily on the front lines, and the Jews being persecuted simply for being who they were. They had no choice. So why should he?

As many families experienced during this time, a husband and father was ripped from the comfort and serenity of the family home and thrown into dire situations. Bloodshed, terror, artillery fire, the sound of explosions, dirt and sleepless nights, these were all familiar situations for soldiers in every guise. It was no different for Gilbert, and it all became his new reality; one he had to grow familiar with very quickly indeed.

Once the drafting was complete, he joined the US Navy as a navy dentist. Now, Gilbert could have swayed his duty; he could have stayed home, hiding behind his status and power as a professional man, but that was never part of his fabric. Gilbert was a strong and capable man, a man of honor and duty. He would never stand by and avoid doing his bit simply to live a more comfortable life at home.

For Eleanor, news of Gilbert's drafting to the Navy hit hard. She was at home alone in Santa Monica, looking after two young girls. What would she say when her girls asked where daddy was? How would she explain that he was away fighting in a war? How could she tell them that they might never see him again if the worst did happen? How could they possibly understand?

During WWII, women were made of grit and grace. They were suffering inside, dying inside even, but they had to put on a brave face and pretend that everything was okay. If they didn't, they would succumb to their swirling emotions, and they may never resurface from the darkness. So that's what Eleanor did – what other choice did she have? She had to stay strong for her daughters and she had to do what she could to keep Gilbert's spirits up, despite the crippling distance between them.

TERROR ON THE HIGH SEAS

Just because Gilbert wasn't in the immediate trenches of the front line didn't mean he was safe. Far from it. Serving as part of the US Navy put him at extreme risk every single second of every day. On the high seas, there was nowhere to hide. If an attack happened, it was all hands on the literal deck to fight for their lives. The sea was a harsh place, even during peace time, but when you add in weapons, it became deadly.

However, despite the apparent danger, Gilbert tried his best to be positive, knowing that if he could express his regular demeanor to Eleanor and the girls, at least they would feel more comfortable.

In that case, a load would be taken off his mind and he knew they would be okay.

Eleanor was a strong woman, but even the strongest of women were tested during the war.

The problem with being at sea is communication. Back then, there were no phones and letters took forever to be sent and replied to. When you add sea into that mix, everything is ten-times worse; soldiers could only receive letters once they docked at port, and letters they wrote while out at sea could only be posted at port too.

Yet, that didn't stop Gilbert and Eleanor from keeping the roaring flames of their love alive through the means of the written word. Throughout two long, desperately lonely years, the couple swapped letters, sharing their desperation at being apart, their lives during the war, and their hopes for the future. They desperately hoped that by talking about the days to come, they would materialize and not disappear in the so-called glories of fighting a war.

Gilbert didn't see any glory in this war. All he could see was desperation and loss.

However, Gilbert was clearly a man who loved to tell a story and that certainly comes through in his letters. On one occasion, he describes in great detail a typhoon that hit while they were moored in Okinawa. It was September 1945, and the weather predicted a storm, yet nobody quite expected it to be at such a magnitude.

Gilbert describes how the sea lurched and swayed, how the boat flung from side to side, and how they were all terrified of the ship being destroyed before the calm of morning arrived. It's clear that Gilbert found speaking in such detail a way of coping. He knew that by doing so, he was helping to paint a picture in Eleanor's mind and that she would feel much closer to him as a result. Perhaps it also made him feel that she was right there with him, offering at least some comfort during the long days and nights.

ELEANOR'S TURMOIL

While Gilbert was right in the heart of battle, Eleanor was fighting her own demons at home. Being so far away from her beloved husband and not knowing if he would return was taking a serious toll on her. As mother to two young girls, she didn't want to show her worry or fear that they would pick up on, but sometimes it was impossible to manage. She would often disappear into another room to take a deep breath and try to keep the tears that threatened to flow at bay.

During Gilbert's absence, Eleanor worked as a substitute teacher in the city. She tried her best to maintain some kind of normalcy for the children in her classes, knowing that many of them were without their fathers. In some cases, perhaps a few of those children would never see their fathers again. It was a sobering and depressing thought that kept Eleanor awake at night, but Gilbert's many letters kept her spirits as high as possible.

Prior to the war, the couple had lived a charmed life. As a dentist, Gilbert made sure the family was comfortable and spent a lot of time together. Yet worldwide events had turned everything upside down and forced them to endure lonely nights apart, constant worry, and a yearning that words simply couldn't express.

It didn't help that Gilbert was moving around a lot, something you would expect when posted to the Navy. He spent time in Eniwetok, Ulithi, the Philippines, and Okinawa. Despite the constant movement and the extreme distance, Eleanor was never away from Gilbert's mind.

His letters were vivid, vibrant, and always full of love. He always used to open the letters with 'Dearest Eleanor' and tried his best to pick out small details that would brighten her day in some small amount.

In one particular letter he explained how it was really hot outside and he wished it would rain. He talked about how he thought the war would end soon, but probably not until mid-1946. He documented how he thought the department was run poorly and that he wanted to move up in rank, to captain's commissioner and nothing less.

Even in the desperate state of war, Gilbert was determined and focused. Eleanor often wished he wasn't, so he could have returned home sooner, but that wasn't the man she married, and despite the distance and the loneliness, she was fiercely proud of her husband.

IT'S ONLY WORDS?

How many times can you tell someone that you love them before the words start to lose their shine?

It's something to ponder. After all, some people believe that the more you say something, the less it means. But for couples ripped apart by the rigors and desperation of war, words were all they had. No matter how many times Gilbert and Eleanor said, "I love you," it never lost its shine. In one particular letter, Gilbert mentions that he hadn't said those important three words lately, but it was simply because words failed him. He was sick of using those words and not being able to follow them up with a hug and a kiss, to see the look on her face, and that familiar twinkle in her eye.

The longing tore them apart, but they stood resolute in their love for one another. Gilbert often said that rather than saying those three words, he would prefer she was beside him and that she could see his love in his actions. He was a clear believer in 'actions speak louder than words.'

Yet, it was clear that despite the distance and the worry, there was still a very strong connection between them. In one particular letter, Gilbert wrote, "You know, honey, you still aren't yourself and I can tell very easily." When you've been with someone for so long, even when you're far apart, you can tell when something isn't quite right. Even through words on a page, Gilbert could read that Eleanor was struggling. She tried her hardest not to let it show, but the twinkle in her personality was dulled because the man she loved wasn't by her side.

For all his status as a professional man, Gilbert never feared showing his love to Eleanor through his letters. Intermingled with mundane chat about movies and dreams, aching wishes and desires were communicated. Swinging from topic to topic, it's clear to see that neither could hold back how they really felt – they were desperate, alone, wishing and hoping. Amongst all of this, Eleanor was trying to keep any sense of worry away from her two young girls.

THE TURNING OF THE TIDE

And then the day came.

After two years of longing, waiting, and wishing, the terror was over.

Just like that.

Gilbert was honorably discharged from the US Navy in June 1946 and returned home to Santa Monica, to be beside his beloved Eleanor and his two daughters, Linda and Norma. Upon his leaving, he was given the rank of Lieutenant, something he was extremely proud of. Of course, Eleanor was bursting with pride at what her husband had achieved, but more than anything, she was greatly relieved to have him home.

During those two long years, Gilbert wrote more than 500 letters to Eleanor. The most astonishing thing is that Eleanor kept them all, neatly folded and preserved for the day when her love would return home to her.

When Eleanor passed away, a devastated Gilbert wanted to destroy the letters, preferring to keep the memories of his dear wife in his heart and mind, but their daughter, Linda had other ideas. Desperate to preserve the special love story her parents shared, she wanted to let the world understand the extreme trials and tribulations they had gone through.

After all, you don't see many couples enduring half of what Gilbert and Eleanor went through and remaining together. Theirs is a story of a charmed life turned upside down, and a man who wanted to do the right thing and fight for his country and the freedom of those who weren't in a position to do so. His family were bereft in his absence, but the love they shared was tested a million times in those days and never broke.

These days, you can read Gilbert's beautiful letters to Eleanor in a blog their daughter, Linda put together, documenting their love story. She regularly updates the blog with excerpts from the letters and details of her father's service in the Navy. Perhaps this is her way of keeping her parents' extraordinary love story alive.

5

DEAR JOAN – TONY & JOAN

How do you get to know someone inside and out?

Is it through speaking to them day and night in person? Being around them at work, or living with them and knowing all their small habits? Some say you never really know a person until you've been away on vacation with them and see their good and bad sides mingling together into one.

These are all ways to find out more about a person, but most of the time, we don't speak our real feelings or show what is inside our hearts. We hold things back, either out of fear of judgement or because we simply don't think it's the right thing to say.

However, some situations in life force us to be vulnerable. We have no choice but to open our hearts and say what we are feeling because otherwise, we'll never feel like the other person understands us completely. Distance has a habit of causing misunderstandings, yet when you open yourself up and speak what's in the deepest depths of your soul, nothing is misunderstood. It's all there, laid out for the other person to absorb.

Tony Ross was a young soldier serving in the British Royal Air Force (RAF). Like most young men of his age, Tony was focused on doing his duty, but lived every day wondering what life would be like if the war hadn't happened. Would he have met someone special? Would he be married? What job would he be doing? Would he be a father by now? What would his children look like?

Tony managed to push these thoughts aside and focused on his work as part of the RAF. The nature of his posting meant that he could be sent to any part of the world at a moment's notice, and the uncertainty weighed heavily on his mind. That's why it came as a huge relief when he met a young woman and instantly clicked with her.

Finally, something positive to think about.

Was it a distraction? At first, maybe. But from there, something special grew.

A CHANCE MEETING

During a period of training in the UK, Tony Ross met Joan Charles. Their meeting was completely random, and you could argue, completely left to chance.

Stationed in Blackpool as part of the RAF, Tony was out walking with a friend one evening and they passed two young women. His friend was a lot more forward than him and called out a greeting to the women. Tony was mortified, but forgot this embarrassment when one of the women, Joan, invited them for coffee in her home. Joan knew her parents would welcome them with open arms, being huge supporters of the armed forces.

They didn't know each other, they had no mutual friends, but it seemed that somehow, fate had intervened and pushed them into each other's lives. Of course, decorum of the time dictated that once you met a young woman, you couldn't simply voice your intentions and let her know that you wanted to court her. So, Tony took his time, and spoke at length to Joan whenever he could.

But then the unfortunate news came that he would be posted to North Africa as part of his service. The two had only met briefly and still barely knew anything about one another, but Tony was keen to keep the feeling of hope and light that Joan provided him with, so he took her address and vowed to write to her whenever he could.

In private however, he rued his luck. He'd finally met someone he liked, only to be snatched away from her, stationed on the other side of the world!

Of course, Joan was feeling apprehensive and worried about Tony's posting. Even though she didn't know too much about this man, she felt there was something special about him. He had a good heart, and she could see that although he was firm in his intention to do his duty, he craved a normal, settled life.

Yet Joan wasn't a woman who was likely to sit around waiting for a man she'd only just met. She was a driven and determined woman herself, volunteering with the Red Cross to help the war effort. In fact, Joan was part of the famous Donut Dugout Truck, a group of Red Cross volunteers who offered to travel overseas as part of mobile clubs, called 'club-mobiles.' The aim was to provide a little home comfort to servicemen with food, a little entertainment, and a home connection.

Joan often talked about her work with the Red Cross, clearly proud of what she was doing and how she was doing her best to help out wherever she could.

CONNECTING VIA THE WRITTEN WORD

Tony's first letters to Joan were shy and simple. Joan's letters followed suit. After all, the two barely knew each other and had only met a few times by chance. But, as time went on, they started to open up a little more and allowed themselves to be vulnerable. Perhaps the rigors of the time exhausted them to the point where they could no longer hold up a protective shield and the walls came tumbling down.

Tony experienced more and more violence during his time in the RAF and the worries he faced as he saw extreme hurt and bloodshed terrified him to the core. Joan's reassuring presence in his life calmed him and allowed him to focus. She was a gentle and serene light in his life. He dreamed of the day when he could put all of this to one side and simply focus on the simpler things – being with Joan was starting to become a major part of his thoughts.

Speaking about everyday things seemed to help them at first, but their feelings were evident after only a few weeks. Sometimes, reading the inner workings of a person's mind via the written word is enough to cause a flame to flicker and burn. For Joan, knowing that Tony could be injured or worse was a terrifying thought. Through her work with the Red Cross, she knew that anything could happen at any time. Yet, she did her best to push those thoughts out of her mind and focus on what she needed to do.

SECRETS? WHAT SECRETS?

It's hard to imagine the fear and longing when someone you're starting to become very attached to isn't by your side. You want to learn more about this person, you want to understand their likes and dislikes, and you are keen to know about their childhood, their family, and the people in their lives who are important to them.

These types of conversations aren't easy to have when the person isn't in the same room as you. You're not sure how to broach subjects that might cause upset – not everyone has an idyllic childhood and a simple question can easily set them off on a dark path. So, writing letters about everyday musings was a chal-lenge for the two at first. Joan wanted to immerse herself in Tony's world and learn every small thing about him, but how could she ask personal questions of someone who was so far away and of whom she knew so little about?

She needn't have worried. Tony wasn't a shy man, despite his initial reserved approach to writing. He answered any question Joan asked and threw in some of his own. They talked at length about everyday subjects, including the war, the weather, their pasts, and what they hoped for the future. At first, they dare not speak about a possible future together – being so bold was something neither wanted to risk, but as time went on, it was clear that their close bond was growing to the point where there were no secrets between them.

A budding friendship had turned from a close connection into a burning love. Joan started to crave Tony's presence beside her, even though she had never had such a closeness with him before. None of it mattered because she felt like she knew him inside out. It was almost as though the two had shared a deep love before his enlistment in the RAF. Were they fated to meet? Was it destiny? Perhaps they had met in a former life, and this was a deep connection rekindling.

The nights were long and cold as Joan wondered how Tony was. Despite the fact they wrote to each other constantly, it seemed like an age between letters; the postal service wasn't the fastest outside of global war, and inside it, everything slowed to a snail's pace, sometimes stopping altogether. This did not help Joan's growing unease.

In one letter, Tony said "Thousands of miles apart and we became closer and closer until there were no secrets between us." The letters they sent back and forth brought them more closer together than any in-person meeting ever could. Their conversations showed their hearts, their true personalities, and their values. They connected in a way they probably never would have if they hadn't been forced into this terrible position.

POURING OUT THEIR HEARTS

Throughout the back-and-forth letters between Joan and Tony we can easily see the timeline of their relationship. At first, they were tentative and held back – they didn't want to say too much but you can sense the underlying determination to find out more. Tony desperately wanted to keep the connection alive as a way to keep hope in his life. Joan was worried about the man she'd just met, and wanted to keep his spirits up, despite his posting overseas.

But as they talked, you can see those walls falling. After a short while, there was no beating around the bush – they said whatever they wanted to say. They were young and full of enthusiasm and, despite the thousands of miles that stood between them, they were keen to keep that flickering flame alive.

You can almost see the karmic connection. The two had a lot in common and shared the same vision of a post-war Britain. Joan talked a lot about her volunteering and the things she saw. Tony tried his best to shield the worst news from Joan but also did his best to be as transparent about his service as possible. Joan talked at length about the frustrating bureaucracy she felt in her work with the Civil Service. In turn, Tony talked about how challenging life was in the desert and how he was given more responsibilities as time went on.

The dreams of the two were evident, but those dreams went from individual ideas to a longed-for future in the arms of one another. Then finally, on February 25, 1944, Tony confessed his true feelings for Joan in a poem. Thrilled to receive his confession, Joan's heart soared, and she finally allowed herself to dream of a future with the man she'd come to know so well.

Within her busting joy, she was forced to push away the worry that she would never actually get to kiss Tony or feel his arms around her. Joan was conflicted and grew even more frustrated at the distance between them.

LOVE COMES IN THE MOST UNEXPECTED WAYS

It's true that falling in love is a process and it always requires us to be in the presence of the other person. We believe that unless we are by their side, there's no way to understand them and feelings cannot grow. Instead, we believe that what we feel isn't real. Back then, it was still a process, something which needed time to grow, but circumstances changed the whole situation, pushing feelings to the forefront much faster. Some may say it wasn't possible to love someone you haven't spent time with, but the connection is still there.

Tony and Joan didn't listen to negative ideas about their budding romance. Pushed together by fate, the two stayed in constant contact as a way to keep a sense of hope and light in their lives. But they provided far more than that for one another.

Sometimes you get to know the other person better when it's just words. No facial expressions, no body language confusion, no expectations, or worries about what they might think. Just words on a page that can't be confused and can easily be read back again and again.

There is nothing to hide behind when words are down on a page. You can't delete them and you can't press 'unsend' on the message. It's there for life, and once you've sent that letter, there's nothing you can do to get it back. It's about bravery and being willing to show someone what you feel.

Sometimes love just happens by chance. You don't plan it and you don't expect it. When you allow someone to see the real you, you allow the walls to fall down, and you open yourself up to a world of opportunities. All of this makes your bond stronger because there is nothing there but you – the real you. You're not pretending to be something you're not out of fear of being rejected. The other person is right there, pouring their heart out at the same time.

We can and should take real hope from Joan and Tony's story. Even a chance meeting and a follow up letter can lead to true love if you are brave enough to be who you are and not hold anything back. Even through the terrifying rigors of war, Tony could think of only Joan. Her letters kept him alive, gave him hope that this ordeal would one day be over, and that he could hope for a better future.

The more she wrote to him, the more Tony started to see Joan as a permanent part of his life and a huge part of his future. And a huge part she was! They remained together long after the war ended. None of this would have happened if they weren't brave enough to speak their hearts on paper. Just one letter can be all it takes to start an epic love story, just like that of Tony and Joan.

6

A CHANCE CORRESPONDENCE – LELAND & LETTY

L ove is the brightest thing in life. Nothing burns as strong as a love that endures the darkest times in life, like death, war, longing, and disappointment. None of it can dull the flame that burns in the heart of someone truly in love.

But love sometimes begins in strange ways, often by sheer chance or total coincidence.

During World War II, nothing was conventional. How can you follow the so-called norms of life when everything is upside down? War changes everything. It extinguishes hope and causes darkness to spread where there once was light. It's a parasite, growing and infecting everything and everyone around it.

But the war generation never let it get them down. We could certainly learn a thing or two from their spirit – they were brave and nothing could sway them from achieving what they wanted out of life. For sure, they compromised and understood that some things simply weren't possible, but distance, fear, the risk of injury, and longing never stopped them from loving each other, even over the miles.

Leland Duvall worked on a farm and was happy with his lot in life. He never asked for too much and did his best to smile every day. He worked hard, did what he had to do, and dreamed of a big future. Yet, when the US joined World War II, Leland, like so many others, received his draft to go and fight.

It was a shock, even though people knew the war was coming. Going from an idyllic countryside life to a battlefield filled with the stench of death wasn't exactly in his plans, yet, like everyone else of fighting age, Leland had no choice. He was torn at leaving the farm, taking in every small detail before he got on the train to leave. He did his best to commit every small thing to memory so he could remember it during the dark days to come.

He was under no illusions – he knew there would be plenty of dark days ahead.

Leland left for basic training in California in March 1942 but a chance meeting on the train gave him plenty of food for thought. He found himself sitting opposite a man he knew from back home in Arkansas. This man was engaged to a local woman named Letty and, despite never admitting it, Leland had always had a crush on young Letty.

She was vibrant, fun, and beautiful in his eyes. Yet she belonged to someone else, and he never allowed himself to dream of a future where she would be his. Being polite was always in Leland's nature, so he made light-hearted conversation with the man, who was also on his way to draft training. In that polite conversation, Leland enquired whether he was still engaged to Letty. He figured that he had nothing to lose by asking, after all, he was on his way to war.

The answer he received shocked him, but then gave him hope.

They were no longer together. Letty was a single woman.

Leland thought about this for a few days, but in desperate need to take his mind off the fate in front of him, he decided to throw caution to the wind and write to Letty. On top of that, he was also furious that his chance at a future with Letty was thrown completely out of the window as he made his way to war. The phrase 'bad luck' wasn't even suitable but was certainly how Leland felt at hearing the news.

LETTY'S SURPRISE

Letty Jones was from Pottsville, Arkansas, and she had no idea that young farmhand Leland had a crush on her. She always knew him to be a polite, friendly young man, often smiling whenever she saw him.

When the first letter dropped on her doormat, she was shocked, but read to the end with excited anticipation. Feeling a little down after splitting up with her fiancé, Letty was flattered by the letter she received from Leland, even though it didn't mention his feelings.

However, Letty wasn't an unintelligent girl – she knew that a man didn't write a woman for no reason! Could it be that Leland had unconfessed feelings for her?

Letty knew Leland well enough but was still anxious to find out more about him. A keen writer, Letty wrote letter after letter to Leland, always replying straightaway when she received correspondence from him, and doing her best to keep his spirits up.

At first, their letters were purely platonic. They talked about life, the rigors of war, and what was going on back home in Arkansas. Yet, as time went on, their letters became increasingly heartfelt and intimate. They knew they were in a sticky situation, and there was no denying the fact that neither had any idea whether they would ever be together in person, but rather than focusing on the negatives, they chose to look at the positives.

It's a remarkable mindset to have when surrounded by so much destruction. It's not easy to be positive in the face of war, no matter whether it's on your own doorstep or thousands of miles away. Leland was right on the frontlines, moving from place to place, and facing untold horrors on a daily basis. Letty's positive attitude did wonders for Leland and whenever he received one of her heartfelt letters, his heart soared.

From bombed-out buildings to military hospitals, Leland never missed a chance to write to his crush, who was fast becoming his love. He was brutally honest about what was happening, but always did his best to shelter Letty from the worst of it.

CHARM, WIT, & PLENTY OF LOVE

How can a person stay so upbeat when dealing with violence on a daily basis? How can someone remain positive when the man they've fallen in love with is thousands of miles away, possibly never to return?

Somehow the starstruck lovers managed to do all of this and more. Focusing on humor and attempting to raise their spirits, Letty always avoided talking about how much she missed Leland. She figured it wouldn't help him and instead, she told him stories that always made him laugh. Doing so helped her to remain positive and she knew that was all she could focus on – being pulled under by fear and worry simply wasn't an option.

On Leland's side, his letters were a constant source of amusement to Letty. Facing untold horrors daily, Leland's writing style was always lighthearted and charming. Yet, he did allow himself to wander into "I miss you" territory once or twice. It was impossible not to. He was a man who couldn't help but speak his heart, and that's exactly what pushed him to write to Letty in the first place!

Yet, the conversations they had were random. You could argue that it was a way of making up for lost time; they built upon their bond with stories about their childhoods and personal notes they wanted to share. At one point Leland went into the rather worrying territory of speaking about Letty's weight! A brave man indeed!

THE DARKNESS OF WAR SETS IN

Leland was fighting in the Normandy invasion and even the slightest bit of history will tell you how brutal and bloody this battle was. One letter written just minutes before going into fight states, "I just have five minutes to write this, so please don't expect me to say more than "I love you" and please keep writing."

Even when facing the very worst of life, perhaps staring death right in the eye, Leland was focused on Letty and desperate for her to continue writing to him.

Thankfully, Leland survived the Normandy invasion, yet the mental scars were deep. Facing such terror was far from his calm life on the farm in Arkansas, and he often longed to be back there, dreaming of a happy and positive future. Yet, he also reminded himself that if it wasn't for that fateful meeting with Letty's former fiancé, he would never have found the bravery to write her a letter. Then, he would never have fallen so deeply in love with the woman he had a mere crush on.

In the meantime, Letty's feelings had grown too. She was often terrified of the thought that Leland wouldn't return home. Desperate to be by his side and never let him go again, she waited daily for the postman to arrive. In-between receiving replies, Letty kept writing her own letters and sending them whenever she could. While she couldn't hold Leland in an embrace, she could do everything to try and keep his spirits up. It was all she could do, so she dedicated herself to doing it as well as she could.

Terrified that Letty would worry about him, Leland did his best to reassure her that everything was fine. Of course, it was far from fine, but he was alive and that was all he could hope for.

LOVE ENDURES EVEN THE DARKEST OF TIMES

The war came to an end. For so many couples, one half never returned, and those embraces were never completed. Yet for Leland and Letty, the dream came true.

They did finally embrace. They did finally cement their love in person, never to be broken apart again.

After the war, Leland became an accomplished writer, using all of his charm and wit to entertain his audiences. After all, he'd had plenty of practice when writing so often to Letty!

It's remarkable to see how positive Leland was even when facing such terror and horror on a daily basis. We can only assume that Letty was the one who kept his spirits alive, and because he never wanted her to worry (although she always did), he forced himself to always see the glass as half full and never half empty.

Through the casual conversations in their letters, you can easily see how much they missed one another. For Leland, the crush he was nursing when he left Arkansas, became a full-blown love affair he could never have predicted.

Through all the bloodshed and death, many believed that nothing positive could come out of the war at all. For sure, justice was at stake, but that couldn't keep lovers and families warm at night when thinking about their lost loves. Yet, in the darkness, there is always a flicker of light. For Leland and Letty, circumstances had pushed them together to the point of realizing that love was just around the corner.

Even in the darkest days of war, Leland knew how important it was to remind Letty that he loved her. He never wanted her to go a day without being told and even when their friendship was platonic and only just starting to grow, the way he wrote his words still said so much, without actually saying it at all.

When we are fearless in love and place faith in the universe, wonderful things can happen. Love can endure all things, even the very worst moments in war. Leland and Letty's love certainly shows this to us.

They were brave and fearless. They trusted that one day they would be together. They faced darkness like no other, but never allowed it to dim the light that had been lit the moment Leland sent that first letter to Letty.

After all, if you don't try, you'll never know what could be.

7

ENDURING LOVE – ARTHUR & MIRLA BANCROFT

Our next story takes us to Australia, to a couple who endured uncertainty and the darkest times possible, all while growing their love through the written word.

Young love is extreme, exciting and often the cause of many lost appetites. But young love also relies on regular presence, sneaked looks, and secret kisses. For our next couple, those heady days of exciting young love were unconventional – all because they never got the chance to try it the traditional way.

Arthur Bancroft was a striking man. He had a sharp wit and a good sense of humor, but perhaps it was his flaming red hair which caught the attention of the young Mirla. All the other girls didn't seem to care for Arthur, but there was something about him that Mirla simply couldn't stop thinking about. Of course, a young woman of the time shouldn't admit to such thoughts, so she kept their connection as platonic as possible, being friendly and joking whenever they met.

You see, the best love stories often start from very small beginnings. It's not usually a major outpouring of love or huge, grand gestures of affection. It's often about small, slow-burning attraction, which perhaps neither party really understood at the time. For many, that's how long-lasting love is born.

Mirla fell for Arthur's cheeky smile, and she was also taken with the fact that he was considerably taller than her. He made her feel safe and feminine. But Mirla was only fourteen years old, and she was only just becoming aware of boys at the time. They used to talk about sports, something they both enjoyed, and Mirla often found excuses to talk about his favorite football team, just to strike up another conversation and enjoy his cheeky wit and smile. She found any excuse to talk to Arthur, adoring every second of his attention.

But, like most young people during World War II, budding love was snatched away and tested to the peak by distance, bloodshed, yearning, and fear.

STEALING KISSES WHEREVER POSSIBLE

As the war started to spread across the world, Australia became involved. At that time, Arthur was prime draft age, and when the call came, he packed his bags and decided he would face his duty like a man. Upon hearing that Arthur was going away, Mirla panicked – what if he never returned? She hadn't yet told him how she felt, and she was terrified at the thought he would never understand her feelings for him.

Just before he went away, Arthur asked Mirla if he could write to her, and they instantly became pen pals. He wasn't sent far at first as he went through basic training. This meant that they could still see each other occasionally, and whenever he was given leave from the Fremantle Navy Depot, he would go and see his "pen pal." Whether it was clear to both of them at the time or not, they were becoming much closer as a result of their pen-to-paper musings, and a few of those navy leave trips ended in sneaky kisses.

Those kisses caused Mirla's heart to soar. Firmly in the first flushes of young love, she couldn't get enough of the young man who was quickly capturing her heart. Yet she knew he would soon be gone and memories would be all that were left. At least for now.

Their friends-with-kissing-benefits arrangement caused Mirla to feel like she was walking on air, but whenever Arthur had to go away again, she worried about him tremendously. He was not yet on the front lines, and she had no idea if or when he would be posted far away.

Yet, little did Mirla know that the call would come sooner rather than later. Arthur was sent to the Flinders Naval Depot in Victoria, the next step toward being sent into active combat. It wasn't long before he left the country as part of his service, destined to witness untold horrors and desperation.

Mirla admired Arthur's bravery and determination to do his part in the war effort, but she was worried about his safety. Arthur did his best to keep his letters to Mirla as upbeat and positive as possible; not only because it helped her to worry less, but it also allowed him to keep his spirits up. The more Arthur wrote to Mirla, the more he realized that he was slowly falling in love. At one point, he was so desperate to write to her that he had to scribble his musings down on toilet paper, as he couldn't find any paper!

Mirla knew she liked Arthur, but it wasn't until he was away that she realized she'd fallen in love. As part of the crew on the HMAS Perth, Arthur was due to set sail on Valentine's Day – of all days! Full of the emotion of such a day, Mirla quickly wrote to Arthur, praying he would receive it before he was due to leave. She poured her heart out and told him exactly how she felt. It was as though a weight had been lifted from her shoulders.

But Arthur never received the letter.

LOST IN ACTION

Just a few days after the HMAS Perth had left port, the local newspaper in Western Australia carried the chilling headline, "Japs sink the Perth."

The ship had been caught by the Japanese and was lying in ruin.

Arthur knew that war would be tough, after all, it was war, but just days after being posted, he found himself floating in the freezing water, desperately clinging to his life jacket and calling for help. It was as though he had lost his sense of sight; all he could see was blackness around him, with the occasional gulp of water and a cry for help. Every so often, he would bump up against something, only to realize it was a dead body floating by.

The boat was hit heavily by the enemy and a huge amount of oil poured out into the sea. Arthur could smell the thick, acrid scent in the air, and was reminded not to swallow the water.

Yet Arthur kept himself strong. Even right at that moment, desperately treading water and trying to stay afloat in oil and water, no idea if help would come or not, he forced himself to think positively. Help would come. It had to. He had Mirla to go home to, and this was not the end for him. He refused for this to be the end.

Perhaps optimism should have been Arthur's middle name, because even through the trials and tribulations to come, he always clung to the hope that he would have Mirla in his arms once more.

CLINGING TO DESPERATE HOPE

Mirla had watched enough movies in her life, she knew the odds weren't in their favor, but something deep inside her told her this wasn't the end. She clung onto the hope that Arthur would be found alive, and he would be sent back home to her.

Just eight days after the sinking of the ship, Arthur's parents received a government telegram, informing them that their son was missing in action as a result of enemy aggression. Mirla knew that all she could do was hope and try her best to keep Arthur's parents' spirits up. After all, if anyone would survive, it would be Arthur. She had never met a more positive person in her life and doubted that she ever would again.

In the dark days after hearing of Arthur's disappearance, Mirla clung to her best friend, Nancy, for comfort. She knew that if she stopped for a second, she would allow herself to think too much. So, she kept herself as busy as possible. She prayed every day for positive news about her love and developed a positive mantra that she repeated every single morning: "Arthur is alive and well." The mantra became part of her ingrained routine, and she used it whenever she felt the swirling nausea of fear starting to rise up in her throat.

To keep her mind busy, Mirla worked at MacRobertson-Miller Aviation five and a half days per week and on the days when she wasn't working, she would busy her mind with anything that would stop her from thinking too much; she even started to play tennis.

Mirla often went to see Arthur's parents and have a cup of tea, yet seeing the toll it was taking on them was very hard to bear. Arthur's grandfather in particular was showing visible signs of strain and Mirla did her best to pull their spirits back up and encourage them to have hope. It was through this she realized that if you want to heal yourself, first you need to direct that attention toward healing others.

However, one sunny October morning, Mirla's spirits soared. Sat on the bus going to work, she repeated her usual mantra, telling herself that Arthur was alive and doing well. When she arrived at work, there was a call for her, it was her friend Betty from Freemantle. Betty seemed emotional and Mirla wasn't sure what to make of it. Betty's brother was also missing in action, having been part of the crew on the Perth. Yet Betty had good news – Arthur was alive.

You can imagine that Mirla's regular working day didn't go according to plan! Instead, she jumped on the bus and rushed back home to tell Arthur's parents the good news. She was convinced that Arthur would soon be coming home, and her head filled with all the things she wanted to tell him face to face, without having to rely upon letters that never arrived.

However, Arthur wouldn't be returning home. He had been captured by the Japanese and was a prisoner of war (POW). Mirla and Arthur's parents had no idea where he was, how he was, or if he would be able to return at any point, but Mirla knew that prisoners of war had to be treated in a certain way according to international law, which gave her some peace of mind. She also knew that he if was in a POW camp, he wasn't on the front lines.

To keep her mind busy, Mirla wrote Arthur a long letter, hoping it would reach him and raise his spirits. It took some time, but her heart soared when she saw an advertisement in the newspaper saying that relatives of captured navy personnel could write a letter via the Red Cross in Melbourne. However, she was limited to just 25 words. *25 words?* How could she express her feelings for the man she loved in so few words? She realized that she simply couldn't, so instead she focused on something she knew would bring a smile to his face – the football scores. She ended the letter with "Love, Mirla."

THE LONG & WINDING ROAD

Both Arthur and Mirla struggled to remember a time before the war. It seemed like all their hopes and dreams, everything they enjoyed back then, and all the people they used to spend time with had been affected and torn apart the moment war had broken out and moved closer to Australia's shores.

Both Mirla and Arthur were positive and optimistic people, but even the world's most upbeat people struggled during those dark times. Not being able to see your partner was one thing, but not knowing where they were or if they were okay was something else entirely. Being limited to just 25 words in a letter, there was no time or space for long, heartfelt declarations of love, or explanations of what was going on back home. Mirla was forced to remember Arthur through memories alone, willing the day when he would finally return back home.

Arthur knew the moment he was released, he would hold Mirla in his arms and kiss her with every fiber of his being. He had missed too much; their love affair hadn't even gotten off the ground before he left. They were still in those heady, honeymoon days when everything was fresh and new. It was also their very first love, the type of love that sweeps you off your feet and takes your breath away.

They were robbed of those sweet days of heady passion, just like so many other young couples at the time.

Eventually, Arthur's parents received a telegram from the Australian Navy telling them that Arthur was safe in Allied hands and that he would be returning home soon. Mirla was walking on air. All of those positive affirmations and optimistic thoughts had worked! Her love was finally coming back home and all those long, dark days of desperately trying to stay busy were about to be over.

She wasn't sure exactly when Arthur would be returning, but she knew it was imminent. Mirla started to wonder if he would still be the same or whether his experiences might have changed him. Would he still find her pretty? Would he remember those sweet, stolen kisses they shared before he stepped foot on the ill-fated ship?

She needn't have worried. Three weeks later, Arthur returned to Australia and the moment he saw her, he wrapped her up in a deep embrace and passionate kiss. Of course, he still found her pretty, and despite all the desperate and dark days he had endured, Arthur still remained the cheeky, confident young man he had been before he left.

LOOKING TO THE FUTURE

Five days after returning home, Arthur proposed to Mirla and, of course, she said yes! They quickly set to making plans and choosing where they would tie the knot, but before they had the chance to act on any of those plans, the Navy jumped in and took Arthur away again!

Due to the fact that Arthur had been captured while an active part of the Australian Navy, he was sent to a convalescent home in Melbourne as rehabilitation after his traumatic experiences. Arthur felt fine and wasn't entirely sure why they were sending him away from his parents and his fiancé after being away for so long, but he figured that he wasn't being sent away to fight, so he would just go with it and wait for them to send him home again.

Mirla was furious that after waiting for so long he was yet again sent away, but she was also keen for him to avoid active service after his long absence, so a convalescent home didn't sound so bad. She was also able to visit occasionally, which kept her spirits up.

During his time in Melbourne, Arthur had a lot of time to think, something he would rather not do. Despite his sunny and upbeat persona, anyone would have been scarred by the experiences Arthur went through. He remembered that dark, oil-slicked night, waiting to be rescued as the Perth was attacked. When help came, he questioned whether it was help at all, as the Japanese captured him and sent him to a POW camp. But he was alive and for that, he was thankful.

Arthur's time in the camp was dark and traumatic. It was hard for him to remain positive, but his mind was set on Mirla, and it was the only thing that got him out of bed in the mornings. His optimism never faltered because he knew that their love would see him through. As for Mirla, she never allowed herself to think for a second that Arthur wouldn't return home.

As war in Europe came to an end, Arthur was sent back to Flinders. This didn't please him because it was full of memories of those who he had set sail with and who hadn't returned. Yet, it was clear that the Navy simply didn't know what to do with him. They kept sending him to different places, passing him around, yet now that the war was over, there was no chance of him being sent on any type of mission. He also had many lasting injuries from his time in the POW camp, which eventually allowed him to apply for medical discharge from the Navy.

The nightmare was over. He was finally free to return home and start to rebuild some kind of normalcy. Of course, that also meant that Arthur and Mirla could finally start to make plans for their future and plan the wedding that would cement their lasting love.

Arthur returned to work at the local bank and life slowly started to feel normal again, yet something inside him had changed. He was still the same cheeky, happy-go-lucky guy, but his experiences had turned him into a man who knew that life didn't always go according to plan.

FAMILY IS EVERYTHING

After all the time spent desperately clinging to hope for the future and repeating positive mantras, Arthur and Mirla finally married. Their young love had grown into something much stronger than butterflies and far more enduring than most unions could ever dream of.

Soon, they started a family, and they pushed all thoughts of distance and worry far behind them. Yet, life still wasn't easy for the couple. They had three children, yet in 1990 they tragically lost their youngest daughter to a malignant brain tumor at the age of 37. Arthur often felt that watching their daughter die was far harder than the time he'd spent as a prisoner of war.

Just four years later, their worries resurfaced again, as their second daughter was also diagnosed with a brain tumor, yet worry gave way to relief when the tumor was found to be benign.

Despite all of life's ups and downs, Arthur and Mirla's love never wavered or weakened. When Arthur was missing, Mirla never gave up hope and always believed in her heart that he would return. Even as he sat in a dark cell in the camp, Arthur forced himself to focus on the future he was convinced he would still have, with Mirla firmly by his side. They were both completely sure that their story wouldn't end there and that they were meant to be.

It's hard to imagine holding hope and positivity so close to your heart when deep inside it's breaking into a million pieces. The constant worry and count of the days turns into an endless maelstrom of negativity if you allow it to take hold, but Arthur and Mirla's story teaches us a very important lesson. Whenever life throws you into the fire, you have to fight and keep the future firmly in your mind's eye.

You can choose to give up. You can give in to the swirling mass of negativity and let it drag you under. Or you can take a chance on the light and hope that things will turn out okay. For Arthur and Mirla, their enduring love for one another was stronger and brighter than anything the war could throw at them. And even though their life was still tough after Arthur returned home, they endured everything, because they had each other.

8

THE LORD LED US TOGETHER – RAY & BETTY

W hen you are surrounded by bloodshed, screams of terror, constant fear, worry, and uncertainty, there is little to hold onto that helps you get through another day. Some focus on dreams of the future, even though the nagging doubt in the back of their minds questions whether it will ever come to fruition.

However, for many people, faith is a constant the helps them through the darkest times in life. During World War II, many questioned their faith. They wondered how a war of such magnitude and terror could happen and how God could allow so many people to die. Yet, faith is a complicated thing and for those who hold onto their religion with care and attention, it brings comfort during the hardest times in life.

For Ray Whipps, a young soldier from Portland, USA, his faith was the one thing that allowed him to keep putting one foot in front of the other as he fought the enemy on the front lines. He was deep in the trenches in Normandy, Paris and Belgium. Surrounded by the stench of death and fear, every day was a struggle to remain positive and to keep in mind what he was fighting for. Yet, just like his fellow soldiers, he had no choice – he had to keep going because far too much depended on it.

In truth, the odds were stacked against him. Every day he endured bullets heading in his direction, bombs exploding around him and near misses. But one particular day, one of those bullets didn't miss and he ended up in the hospital with severe injuries.

A NEAR MISS AND A COLLISION WITH FATE

Do you believe in love at first sight?

For Betty, the moment she opened the cubicle curtain and saw a handsome man sitting there reading the New Testament, she felt something she'd never experienced before.

Betty was a nurse in Cherbourg, France, serving as a lieutenant and doing her part in the war effort. Throughout her service, Betty nursed several soldiers back to health, however, many were lost. Her faith kept her strong in the face of such trauma and upset, and yet somehow, when she saw Ray, she couldn't explain the strong connection she felt.

The ironic thing is that Ray wasn't even supposed to be in Cherbourg. Having been injured in artillery fire in the Hürtgen Forest in Germany, the medics were supposed to airlift him to England, but terrible fog made it impossible. He was put on a hospital train and found himself in France, at the 167th General Tent Hospital, around three miles outside of Cherbourg. You could say it was a strong twist of fate.

Betty had never seen a soldier reading the New Testament before, at least not after being so terribly injured in combat. Many questioned their faith at that point, rather than moving closer toward it and holding it close to their hearts. Betty asked the man if he was a Christian and after he replied that he was, they sat and talked about their faith for a while.

Ray knew that he wasn't supposed to fraternize with Betty due to their ranks, and they were never alone for long. Yet, something about the kind-hearted nurse pulled at his heart strings. Her expert care quickly nursed him back to health and he was soon able to walk on crutches. At this point, they would go to the local church together and pray, they would go to the movies showing at the local theater and some days they would go and enjoy Bing Crosby together. These were the only times they were allowed to be alone.

Ray knew he was starting to fall in love with Betty when he felt jealous of her caring for the other soldiers. She gave them the same care and attention as she had given to him, and he questioned whether he was reading too much into the situation, yet something told him he wasn't. There was a careful twinkle in her eye whenever she was with Ray, and he couldn't explain it in any other way.

AN IMPORTANT QUESTION

Throughout the weeks that Ray spent in the military hospital, he grew closer and closer to Betty. She couldn't wait to go and see him in the mornings, enjoying caring for the handsome soldier and trying to push away the knowing worry that he would soon be discharged and head back out into combat.

But Betty knew the game of war all too well. After all, she was an army personnel and she understood that, once recovered, there would be no respite for Ray. It was something he might not have chosen for himself, had war not knocked on their doors, but he had to do his bit and for that, Betty respected him. Yet, it didn't mean she wasn't filled with worry.

When Ray's condition improved to the point of him being discharged, he had one important question for the kind nurse to whom he probably owed his life – and his heart. "If we both make it out of this alive, will you marry me?"

For a second, Betty was speechless. But then she gathered her thoughts - she loved this man and when the war ended and they were reunited, they would be husband and wife. She said "Yes!" and the two began writing to each other as Ray was once again posted back to active combat.

As Ray left the hospital, Betty carried on tending to the wounded soldiers and giving them all her care and attention. She found the distraction was helping her to avoid thinking about where Ray might be and what he might be going through. The fact that he had been injured had made him understand his own mortality, and as Betty dealt with life and death every single day, she knew all too well of the terrible perils of war. Yet, she knew there was only one thing she could do – trust in God and hold onto her faith. She was strong in her resolve and knew that Ray would return to her, and they would be married.

Ray was posted to Nancy in France, and he took the officers' candidates exam. This meant he would be promoted to officer, and he would be able to 'fraternize with' and marry Betty. The fact that she was a lieutenant was currently a problem and certainly meant that when, not if, the war ended, there could be an issue in getting permission to be open about their relationship, let alone marry.

Thankfully, Ray passed the exam and was due to go to office candidate school in Paris. However, a cruel twist of fate interrupted his plans once more, as on the 1st of April 1944, he was captured by the Nazis and was taken to the Stalag VII-A prisoner of war camp in Moosburg. The camp was the largest of its kind in Nazi Germany and was full to the brim with captured soldiers. Conditions were grim, food was scarce, and all prisoners were malnourished, full of lice and fleas, while suffering from extreme depression.

Ray's faith was tested once more, but he refused to let his resolve suffer. Whenever he felt that he couldn't take anymore forced labor, torture, or darkness, he kept Betty's face in his mind's eye and remembered the answer to his question. Her "Yes!" meant that the future would be brighter than anything the Nazis could throw at him. It was the only thing he had to hold onto, and he kept hold as tightly as he possibly could.

A FUTURE LOST?

Betty regularly wrote to Ray, but the letters she sent were always returned, stating 'MIA,' missing in action. With every returned letter, her worries grew. She knew if he'd been captured by the Nazis he would be in the middle of a very grim situation, with no clue when or if he would ever be released.

The letters continued to be returned, until one gray day, it no longer said MIA, but KIA – killed in action.

Betty's heart sank. The man she had fallen for, even though she had never spent much time with him alone, had been snatched from her so cruelly. She knew that Ray would have fought with all his might and that he would have prayed until the very last second for his future to continue and for him to be in her arms again.

Yet something told her not to give up yet.

She couldn't quite explain the feeling, but she wasn't willing to let it go. Despite the KIA firmly stamped on the letter returned to her, she hadn't seen an obituary or a body, and until that moment, she refused to give up hope. She felt that God was telling her to hang in there, that perhaps this wasn't the end of the road for their budding love affair. After all, they were due to be married!

The people around Betty gave her looks of pity and offered their sympathy, yet she simply smiled tightly and carried on with her day. She clung to her faith with every ounce of her being and carried on caring for the injured soldiers who came through the hospital doors every single day. From April until September, she had no idea if he was missing, dead, or alive, but she simply focused on the only thing she could control – caring for the injured and sick.

Ray's life in the camp was nothing short of miserable. As people died around him, he closed his eyes and kept remembering Betty's features. The more he could remember, the closer he was to her. Giving in simply wasn't in Ray's DNA; his faith kept his mind on the positive, even when everything around him was dark and dismal. For most, there was nothing worth living for inside the camp, and a lot of his fellow soldiers were giving up. Even Ray had no idea if anyone back home knew if he was alive or dead.

Yet, one fateful day, another letter returned to Betty. She was confused at first, because if Ray was, as they said, killed in action, how would letters still be heading back to her.

Ray wasn't dead. He had been given the wrong army post office number and Betty's letters were mistakenly thought to be for another soldier – a soldier who had unfortunately been killed in action.

There were no words to describe Betty's relief. It was as if a huge wave had rushed over her and left her legs weak. She was lightheaded with joy and couldn't remember a single second in her life to date when she'd felt such giddy joy. Ray was alive! God had heard her prayers and told her not to give up. They were going to be reunited after all!

Betty's devotion to her faith was the only thing that had stopped her from giving up on her dream entirely and caving into the sadness and darkness around her. For Ray, he knew that if he hadn't kept his mind focused on prayer and hope, he would have succumbed during his days in the camp and he would have never seen Betty's beautiful face again.

A NEW FUTURE

For most people, hope is all they have to hold onto, yet for those who give everything to their faith, they feel a strength that cannot be explained. Betty and Ray understood that all too well. When they saw each other in person again, for the first time since Ray was released from hospital, they no longer held back. Ray rushed to Betty and held her tightly in his arms. Betty felt her legs go weak and clung onto Ray with all her being. Finally, he was home!

It was at that moment they shared their first kiss, even though in the eyes of the army, their fraternization was still very much frowned upon! However, the war was over, and very few army majors would deny a request from a soldier to marry their true love. The couple finally married on September 29, 1945, in New Orleans, before settling back in Southeast Portland.

They went on to have seven children, eighteen grandchildren, and thirteen great grandchildren. They filled their life with children, love, and laughter, and went on to publish a book outlining their commitment to faith and one another, titled "'Til We Meet Again."

Can you imagine not knowing for sure if the man you had only just met and fallen for would ever be in your life again? Can you imagine being sent back to active combat with the face of the woman you adore seared into your mind? Without the strength of their faith to fall back on, it's possible that Ray and Betty would never have seen one another again.

When World War II was raging, everyone had their go-to thing to help them cope. For some it was simply staying as busy as possible. For others, it was doing their bit for the war effort, or writing to their love as much as possible. Sitting still and thinking too much was not an option, doing so would simply lead you down a path toward desperation and misery, and that was a slippery slope indeed.

For Ray and Betty, even though they were both heavily involved in the army, with Ray in active service and Betty in the medical field, they had no time to sit and think. The hope they both had was rooted deeply in faith, and without that, how would Betty have coped thinking that her love was dead and that she would never have that first kiss?

Sometimes the strength of love and faith are exactly what we need to get through difficult times. Deeply holding onto the hope of a better future can help you overcome whatever life throws at you. For Ray and Betty, that was certainly the case, as they moved toward their true happily ever after.

9

ALL MY LOVE ALWAYS – STEPHEN & AILSA

When a young man is drafted to fight, they have to leave behind everything they've ever known, everyone they've ever loved, and all the hopes and dreams they have for the future. They have no idea if the life they will return to will be the same as the one they had when they left, or indeed if they'll ever return at all.

It's a huge amount of bravery to accept your fate, especially when that fate means fighting for a cause that you never wanted in your life. However, war also means understanding that it's important to be of service. For many young men, that meant going to the war office, putting themselves forward, and leaving their homes for who knows how long.

Stephen Russell was just like those men. He was a young man with his life ahead of him with dreams and hopes he wanted to achieve. He also had his eye on a beautiful young woman named Ailsa back home. Although nothing had happened between the two of them, he certainly hoped that in the near future it would.

But then the war happened.

In 1939, Stephen stepped up and joined the Black Watch 3rd

Battalion in the Royal Regiment of Scotland. Almost instantly, he was posted overseas to Germany, directly fighting on the front lines. He was only twenty-three years old, and like most young men of that age, he was precocious, thought he knew what he was getting himself into. But soon enough he realized that he didn't have the first idea of the realities of war.

Despite his realization, Stephen persevered. He knew that this wasn't what he had hoped for his life, but he pushed through and did his duty anyway.

The only thing that helped Stephen endure years of battle and hardship was penning heartfelt letters back home to his mother and to his new found love, Ailsa.

THE RIGORS OF WAR IN THE WRITTEN WORD

The interesting thing about Stephen's letters home is that we don't get to learn a huge amount about Ailsa's background. We don't know what she did for a job, what she hoped for the future, or much about her family. What we do know however, is that Ailsa was as head over heels in love with Stephen as he was for her. At first, their love grew slowly, flickering like a flame that hadn't yet managed to take hold. However, the longer Stephen was away, absence really did make the heart grow fonder.

You would think that if you weren't yet in a relationship with someone and they went away for several years, the embers would burn out and you'd move on. However, Ailsa wasn't that kind of a person. The letters that Stephen and her penned to one another meant that they came to know each other in a more intimate way than most couples who saw each other every day.

Stephen often wrote about the reality of war, while trying to avoid giving away secrets in his letters. He was careful about how much he said because he was worried about one of his letters being intercepted en route and being opened by the enemy. He was also aware of his seniors reprimanding him for saying too much.

However, Stephen found it therapeutic to talk about the day-to-day grind on the frontlines. In one particular letter to Ailsa, Stephen talked about having to move around from place to place. He expected this to be the case, after all, soldiers don't tend to stay in one place during active war. But he found it hard to keep moving because he could never settle. His life was so upside down with Ailsa so far away that he could never put down his roots.

Stephen always started his letters with "Darling Ailsa," and all his letters were full of vivid description. Whether writing to his mother or to Ailsa, he was careful not to say anything which would cause them to worry any more than they already did, but he also clearly found it as a form of escape to talk openly about what he was going through on a day-to-day basis.

In one particularly descriptive letter, Stephen talked about how he missed the sound of bombs and crashes during the evenings, as when darkness fell, it was always so quiet. When there were "No Germans to shoot at" he found it unsettling, and the darkness and silence felt too earie. He joked about how he has become a killer with a thirst for German blood, but then moved back to tender words of love for his mother and Ailsa, opening up about how he couldn't wait for the war to be over so he could return home and start the future he had dreamed about so much.

LOVE SURVIVES AGAINST ALL THE ODDS

Developing a love affair takes time. You must get to know each other carefully, feel out whether you can overcome the other's faults while embracing their strengths, and of course, there's the physical side of things which allows you to remember every single look and smile. When the person who is quickly becoming the love of your life is stationed on the other side of the continent, deep in the thick of battle, surrounded by gun fire, it's easy to become cynical and convince yourself that love simply isn't meant to be.

However, Ailsa and Stephen never allowed those thoughts to take root. Against all the odds, they focused their minds on the future and convinced themselves that their time would come. Ailsa made it her mission to stay as busy as possible during the time that Stephen was away. Distractions allowed her to push aside the thought of her love fighting and desperately trying to stay alive.

Ailsa also became close to Stephen's parents, after he'd made it very clear in his letters to his mother that he saw Ailsa as the one for him and that once he returned from war, he intended for them to marry.

The odds were stacked against them, but they never allowed themselves to focus on the negatives.

Then, one fateful, dark day, Stephen's parents received a telegram from the army, informing them that their son had been injured, admitted to a German hospital, and was now a prisoner of war. He had suffered a bullet through his right shoulder and shrapnel injuries elsewhere, but he was alive.

For Ailsa and Stephen's parents, it was easy to focus on the fact that Stephen was a prisoner of war, but instead they chose to focus on the fact that his injuries had not been fatal. While he was alive, there was still a strong chance that they would one day be reunited.

For Ailsa, Stephen's incarceration was a source of extreme mixed emotions. On one side, he was a prisoner in enemy hands, but on the other side, he was no longer in active combat. He could also continue to write home, which allowed their love to continue to grow.

You see, when all you have is the written word, there is nothing but raw honesty to rely upon. Anything else is contrived and obvious to the recipient. Ailsa had grown to know Stephen in a way that she could never have managed if he was by her side. She understood his fears and his dreams, his tone of voice and how it changed according to his mood. All of this helped her to understand him better and also allowed her to do everything she could to keep his spirits up through letters.

Of course, being a prisoner of war, the mail service wasn't exactly reliable. Much of the time, letters on either side were lost or arrived extremely late. The days in between were a dark, swirling mass of worry. Yet, every time a letter arrived, there was an overwhelming feeling of joy.

MOTHER, SHE'S THE ONE

On February 20, 1943, Stephen wrote to his mother and talked about his growing love for Ailsa. By this time, Ailsa had been to visit Stephen's parents and the meeting had been a roaring success. This was a huge weight off Stephen's mind as anything else would have made their union extremely difficult.

Stephen talked about how he'd never been surer of anything in his life and that he loved Ailsa with all his heart. He knew they were meant to be and that she was sent to him. He also talked about how it was difficult to stay in touch because letters weren't being received on either side. When his mother asked if he was certain about his feelings, he responded with a resounding "Yes!".

Despite being a prisoner of war and facing terrible conditions every single day, Stephen clearly set his mind on the day when he would be free. He talked about how he was sure that everything would be fine when he returned, and that he was ready to start his life again. He also talked about how he wished he could have made his parents prouder during his stint in the army, as all he had done was "Sit on his arse for three and a half years in Germany!". He also talked about a relative's boils and how he was glad they were improving!

It's this change from serious to lighthearted writing that allows you to see Stephen's character without actually meeting him in person. Such strength and fortitude were common during the war, after all, anything else would have meant death for certain. Yet for Stephen, it was clearly his love and hope for the future that kept him ticking along. The hundreds of letters he wrote home were his way of coping; without doing so, we'd never know if he would've coped as well as he did.

On January 1, 1945, Stephen's frustration was clearly starting to show. He was tired of not being with Ailsa and fed up with letters not making their way to her and back again. The festive season had also made him feel more homesick than ever before. At this point, he realized that after eight years of service, he'd spent five years in captivity, and he missed the normal things in life. He pondered whether he would be able to slot back into life as before, or whether everything would be changed for good.

However, he knew one thing would change and he would soon be a married man. The only thing that kept him going during that long New Year was the knowledge that he could soon hold Ailsa in his arms and feel her heart beating against his. He felt guilty knowing that she was home and worrying about him so much. He knew she was a strong woman, and she was doing all she could to stay busy, but he also knew that she had a kind heart and worried about him endlessly.

In a letter to his mother, Stephen talked about how he worried about Ailsa and how he wasn't sure how else he could reassure her when his own faith was starting to wane. He wrote how sometimes he wondered whether he should tell her not to wait around anymore, that it was not fair to her and she should go and meet someone who could be there for her, but he couldn't bring himself to do it because he loved her and wanted her so badly. He was terrified of anyone else taking his place.

Ailsa would certainly never have allowed anyone else to come into her life because, for her, Stephen was the only one. In their letters, they allowed themselves to talk about their future, including the children they might have and the type of house they'd like to live in. The dream they built together, albeit across miles through the written word, was the only thing that Ailsa had her mind set on.

DESTINY WILL ALWAYS HAVE ITS WAY

On May 8, 1945, the war was officially over. Hitler's suicide one week earlier had started the domino effect and before long, his army fell. Upon news of the allied armies' successes, people flocked out into the streets, singing, dancing, embracing, and celebrating victory. For Stephen, his nightmare was over, and he would soon be released back home. All those years as a prisoner of war were about to end.

For Ailsa, the years of hoping, dreaming, trying not to worry, and staying as strong as possible, were all over. She would soon be a married woman, finally realizing her destiny to be with the man she truly loved.

The days before Stephen's arrival home seemed to drag slower than ever before. The seconds seemed to last for hours! Ailsa spent time with Stephen's parents, preparing for his arrival and awaiting news of a definitive date. When that day came, the feelings were indescribable.

When two people are meant to be, nothing and no one can keep them apart.

No matter how difficult things were for Stephen, even when he was in a dirty cell as a prisoner of war, hungry, desperate for sleep, tired of hearing the screams of fellow prisoners, and wondering whether the endless hours would ever release him, he never allowed his spirit to dampen to the point where his love for Ailsa wavered. She was the golden light that guided him through the darkness and pushed him to keep going.

Even during the most trying of times, Ailsa continued to write back, even when the mail didn't work properly, and letters weren't being delivered.

Love endures all hardships in life, and although many couples never saw one another again once the war was over, Stephen and Ailsa were one of the lucky ones. They went on to marry, start a family, and lived long and happy lives in one another's arms.

Upon discovering his late grandparents' letters to each other during World War II, Ben Smith decided to create a podcast called "Love Stephen." Here, Stephen's letters are showcased to tell a unique and beautiful love story of purity and faith. Between 1939 and 1945, Stephen and Ailsa never allowed themselves to think for a second that they wouldn't be together. Even when things were dark and nothing seemed to work, they knew that they had one another.

10

A REUNION NEVER TO BE – RALPH & BERYL

N ot all stories have the happy ending we hope for. Some go through endless twists and turns before finally being granted with that golden future. But for many during World War II, the last goodbye was over the miles, unexpected, crushing, terrifying and painful.

But love still endures.

Being called to war is no easy task. Even for those who are in active service, the cold reality of being sent to active combat is terrifying and blood-curdling. For those left at home, worrying and wishing the whole thing was over, every day is an endless slog of tears, fear and distractions.

Beryl Williams and Ralph James were a happily married couple from Australia. Having tied the knot on February 21, 1941, the couple were still in the throes of their honeymoon passion when the call came which they had been dreading. Just three months after their nuptials, Ralph joined the Royal Australian Air Force and was sent to Darwin. His task was flying Hudson bombers in active service.

Beryl always knew that there was a strong chance Ralph would be sent away, such was the nature of his military job. She just never thought it would happen quite so soon after their wedding. Yet even years would have been too soon. Despite all of this, Beryl knew that Ralph was an excellent pilot and although she was worried about what may happen to him in the face of enemy aggression, she did her best to stay strong for him.

Ralph felt wretched dragging himself away from his young bride. Their lives together had only just begun and there he was, being pulled away from his new home, new wife and new life.

MAINTAINING SOME FORM OF NORMALCY

It's easy to fall into the trap of writing long, maudlin letters, desperate words of hope and worry, but for Ralph and Beryl, sticking together and talking about their future helped them far more. Constant reassurances of their love for one another got them through the first few dark months. The intimate honesty of their letters showed the clear bond of a newly married couple.

"Always dear, I'll owe you the world for the happiness you have given me since I met you and especially since we've been married," wrote Ralph. His world had changed the moment Beryl had agreed to be his wife. "I'm sure you understand me better than I do myself, so perhaps you understand what I'm trying to say – that I love your body and soul, now and always, so much that the thought of you with me is just torture because we're apart."

Ralph had no problems putting his feelings into words. Many men of the time struggled with endless declarations of love, but for Beryl, the fact that Ralph found it so easy was a comfort. They talked back and forth about their future and what they hoped for once the war was over. They wanted to start a family and be content in one another's arms, without the fear of war getting in the way. For the two of them, this was how they kept some form of normalcy within a very abnormal situation. They knew that they wouldn't be able to see one another in person for a while, and that while could stretch to months or even years. Talking about the day when it would all be over kept them focused on the positive rather than allowing themselves to be dragged down by the endless amount of time that stood between them.

A HONEYMOON INTERRUPTED

Do you think it would be easier to develop a love affair through letters, as many of the couples we've talked about so far did? Or do you think it would be easier to have an established relationship before war breaks out?

For Ralph and Beryl, their strong bond helped them to give one another what they needed, albeit through the written word. Ralph had an uncanny knack of being able to read Beryl's moods through her letters, so he knew whether he needed to lift her spirits or talk about something in particular. For Beryl, she also developed a keen sense of understanding when it came to her husband's needs.

Ralph always did his best to remain upbeat and positive, but the rigors of war were enough to drag even the most optimistic man to his knees. Beryl knew how to talk to Ralph to pull his spirits back up, mostly about the family they would have in the future and all the fun they would have together.

Perhaps the most difficult thing, and something Beryl alluded to several times in her letters, was the fact that they knew what it was like to be in each other's arms. They had felt the warmth of being together, sharing a bed, and enjoying one another's company without the fear of judgement or separation. Being snatched away from each other so quickly after marrying was a cruel twist of fate, but neither could afford to dwell on such a misfortune for too long. Doing so would be a dangerous thing and could cause Ralph to take his eye off the ball, lose focus, and endanger his life in the process.

During Ralph's absence, Beryl returned home to her family. They owned a hotel in Queensland that had become popular with Australian and American servicemen looking for some much-deserved R&R. Beryl had no interest in any of the men she encountered on a daily basis, but it didn't stop Ralph from worrying about her devotion during his time away.

In one particular letter, Ralph enquired if Beryl was okay because she had seemed quiet and unlike herself recently. He knew deep down that she was probably just worried, but he couldn't help but worry about the number of men Beryl was spending her time around and if she had fallen in love with someone else. In some ways, he knew he couldn't have blamed her, after all, her husband was far away with no return date in sight.

Ralph asked Beryl to tell him if she has indeed fallen for someone else because he would rather know. He made it clear that he knew there were some "Jolly fine fellows" at the hotel and perhaps she had found herself feeling a certain way about one of them.

Yet, Beryl would never entertain such a thought. Her mind and heart were firmly with Ralph and, even though she was constantly surrounded by servicemen on leave, not one caught her eye. All she could think about was the day when her husband would return to her. In the meantime, she helped her parents at the hotel, trying her best to stay busy and not to worry.

Ralph's almost psychic connection to Beryl meant he knew when she was worrying more than normal. He constantly reassured her that he couldn't imagine a life without her and that he was as safe as he could possibly be. Alleviating her worries was not easy in the middle of a war, but he told her that if anything did happen and he ended up in the sea, he would still find his way back to her. "Who could stop me coming home to you and if I ever were shot into the sea, I guess I could swim all the way home to you, dearest."

Beryl's ability to stay positive even in the face of terror and fear was admirable. She did her best to show Ralph that his words helped her, hoping that in turn, she could do the same. She was bemused by his thoughts of her falling for another man; how could she ever think of even giving another man a second glance when she had already married the man she wanted to spend the rest of her life with?

She was simply waiting for the day when the war was over so they could carry on where they left off. She was also extremely sure that they would never take one single thing for granted ever again. War has a habit of making you look at what you had before and see it in a new, extremely appreciative light. All couples have difficult times, everyone has faults and quirks that their partner may find irritating at times, but when you're apart, those faults suddenly turn into things that you adore about the other person. Beryl knew she would never allow a small disagreement to derail a second of their future lives together.

She promised herself this.

A LOST LOVE

It's always easier to read positive stories. We want to read the 'happily ever after's' and the heroes' tales. These help us to see life as something we can overcome as long as we stay positive and hope for the best. But reality is quite different.

The reality of war is a massacre.

It's true that some will make it home but it's absolute that they'll forever be changed. The echoes of screams and bloodshed will forever ring in their ears.

For others, their story ends. The darkness overtakes them, and their efforts live on as memories. Their families and spouses, no longer have a future to hope for, instead they're forced to grieve by a graveside.

Beryl remained as positive as she could be for the entire time Ralph was away, but as she went about her day at the hotel with her parents, she received the news. News she had desperately dreaded since the day Ralph left her side.

Her husband would not be returning. Ever.

Just three months after Ralph had written to Beryl asking if she had fallen for someone else, reassuring her desperately of his love, and reminding her that he could never imagine a future without her, he was gone.

Ralph's bomber had suffered a catastrophic engine failure which couldn't be rectified despite desperate efforts. The plane crashed into the Arafura Sea and Ralph was killed on impact.

The news was like a shot through the heart for Beryl. The man she had vowed to spend the rest of her life with, the man she had planned to start a family with and committed herself to, was now gone. He was not coming back, and she hadn't even had the chance to hold him one last time and say goodbye.

In those dark days after learning of Ralph's death, Beryl leaned upon her parents for help and support. At first, she was numb, but then her feelings turned to anger. Her kind and gentle husband had been sent away to fight for a cause that had killed him. Now she was left mourning the love that would never return before they even had a chance to really begin their married life.

THE REALITY OF WAR

You might wonder why we have ended our series of love stories on such a tragic tale. The reason? Because not all love stories end in a happily ever after. Truth be told, these are the minority.

Millions of couples found themselves torn apart during war and while many found themselves back into each other's arms, countless were left to mourn their lost loves.

There is nothing glorious or beautiful about war. There is only loss, terror, death, and endings. A man who goes to war returns changed, whether he will ever admit it or not. It's impossible to view such violence on a daily basis and remain the same. The hope and purity you have before you are sent away disappears the moment you see a fellow comrade die before your eyes.

For those who made it back to their spouses, there were countless more who didn't.

Beryl knew that Ralph would never allow her to mourn for long. While every day felt like the world's biggest effort for a long time after Ralph's death, Beryl tried her best to keep going. However, when she heard the news that the war had ended, she felt conflicted.

The war was over, and the world was free again. Of course, that was amazing news. But at what cost? Her husband was gone and the future children she planned to have with him would never be.

Beryl went on to marry twice more after Ralph's death, but she never had any children. She knew that Ralph would want her to be happy and wouldn't want her to remain alone for the rest of her days. She felt his presence by her side every single day and always thought back to those heady days after they married, when they had no idea of the anguish that was due to come their way.

Beryl never forgot Ralph, just as every single lost serviceman during World War II, or indeed any war, will never be forgotten.

CONCLUSION

Love is different for every couple. Some people don't verbalize their feelings, while others can't help but allow their feelings to roll out of their mouth in a way that move the soul. But one thing remains – love is the strongest emotion on the planet and, no matter what life throws at you, it will endure.

A flickering light in the soulless darkness, love will guide you through the hardest times of your life. All you need to do is trust it.

During World War II, it was very easy to allow your feelings to be clouded by darkness. But you couldn't afford to. After all, that's what the enemy wanted. To force the life and hope out of the people meant demoralizing and knocking down the shield of determination. When you do that, it's easier to win.

The generations that lived through World War II were constantly tested but their mighty spirit held on. We can learn a lot from them even today. Even without the war, the older generations didn't have the same opportunities and freedoms we have today. They certainly didn't have the technology. What they did have was the ability to communicate clearly, to speak their hearts and minds and to refuse to give in.

Love was different back then. It was epic on a grand scale. But that wasn't unusual, it was just how it was.

Take Tony Ross and Joan Charles as a good example. They were in love yet snatched out of each other's arms as Tony was drafted into the war effort, having previously served at RAF Squires Gate Airfield near Blackpool, England. Joan had been evacuated from London and was living in St Annes, working as a civil servant. They were just twenty-two years old, but the couple kept their love alive through writing letters back and forth, not holding back in telling one another how they felt. It was simply what you did back then.

"But love me for love's sake, that evermore thou mayst love on, through love's eternity."

A STRONG MESSAGE FROM EACH STORY

Each story we have told throughout this book has a unique, yet strong message to take forward. These are things we can use in our own lives and lean on when we show our partners affection. You might think that your partner knows you love them, but do they? Everyone has a different love language, be it acts of service, words of affirmation, quality time, receiving gifts, or physical touch.

It's important to know your partner's love language so you can help them feel as cherished as possible.

During World War II, when couples were pulled apart and forced to love over the miles, the only love language they could use was words of affirmation. Quality time was out of the question and physical touch was just a pipedream, pushed away to some longed-for time in the future.

Let's remind ourselves of the key messages from each of our heartbreaking stories.

For Christopher and Bessie, young love burned heavily despite the miles, yet the yearning was almost too much to bear. Bessie could easily have given up waiting and moved on, but her love for Christopher and the hope that they would be married upon his return kept her loyal and waiting. For them, the happily ever after came to be and despite Christopher's rather factual way of writing, he had no problem showing his love when they were reunited!

We learned that love endures all in spite of the hardships in the tale of Lenny and Diana. United in the fight against fascism, the couple knew that there was something bigger to push for. Their united front allowed them to stay true to their roots and keep their love burning. Through all the hard times, they never allowed the flame of their love to dim.

In the heartbreaking tale of Felice and Lilly, we learned that love is love regardless of gender and that it is fierce and worth fighting for no matter what. Despite the constant fear of Nazi persecution, the couple endured everything life threw at them. Even though in the end they were separated, Lilly never allowed Felice's life or their love to be in vain.

Gilbert and Eleanor had a charmed life prior to war being declared, yet despite Gilbert's esteemed profession, he knew he had to go and do his part in the war effort. Love was a constant comfort to Gilbert as he was sent away for years, while Eleanor remained at home looking after their daughters, safe in the knowledge that Gilbert's adoration knew no bounds.

Then we have Tony and Joan, who got to know each other through letters. Sometimes love doesn't have to be familiar, it can be about taking a chance on a stranger that you simply have a good feeling about. When all you have is letters, you allow yourself to pull down your walls and be vulnerable. The constant violence of war is undoubtedly jarring but having a light of love to focus on is a wonderful comfort.

For Leland and Letty, their constant back and forth letters

helped them overcome the distance and build a new bond. Of course, Letty had been engaged to someone else, but upon that relationship ending, Leland found out, took his chance, and wooed Letty with his words! It's pretty remarkable to think that such a love affair could take root with so much distance between them, but that's the amazing thing about love – it doesn't need to be prescribed or follow rules; it will always have its way.

Who is next? Arthur and Mirla, of course. For many months, Mirla faced the possibility that Arthur was dead. Yet, she never allowed herself to believe it completely; she had to focus on the remote chance that he was alive and somehow finding his way back to her. Mirla's positivity was the only thing that kept her from giving in and accepting Arthur's demise. However, we later found that Arthur was not dead and was a prisoner of war. Eventually, he would make his way back to his true love.

Ray and Betty relied upon their faith to see them through the dark times, always looking to the future and dreaming of what would come next. For them, love was trust and endurance, it was a sense of knowing that whatever came next, they would be okay because they had one another.

Stephen and Ailsa's love grew through talking non-stop about everything and nothing. Somehow, Stephen knew that Ailsa was the one for him and his mind focused on them marrying once he returned from service. He wrote letter after letter to his mother, explaining how he had met the love of his life and he was simply waiting for their time to come. He refused to believe for a second that there would be any other outcome.

Then we have Ralph and Beryl. A tragic story of a young love cut short. Having married shortly before Ralph was sent away for active service, their love grew in distance and Ralph developed an almost psychic ability to read his wife's moods through her letters. His love never wavered and never left his mind; it was the one thing that allowed him to stay focused on his job.

However, we know that Ralph never returned home, and Beryl was left to mourn the demise of her dear, beloved husband. Despite the tragic ending, Ralph and Beryl's story teaches us that love has no limits, it is a deep feeling despite risk and worry, even when one half of the partnership doesn't return. Love never dies, and even though Beryl went on to marry twice more, she never forgot her first husband.

IS MODERN LOVE AS EPIC AS WARTIME LOVE?

With all the wonderful tales of love and hope we've read, it makes you question whether modern love really is as deep and epic as love that took place during World War II. While there are certainly some beautiful tales in the world right now, the way we love and interact with those around us has changed beyond measure.

Back during World War II, there was no internet, no messaging apps and no social media. If you wanted to express your interest in someone, you had to do so in person, and that often meant approaching her father to ask for permission!

Courting was an entirely different proposition compared to today's dating world. Everything was slower, measured, and careful. Whispered words of affection were often as spicy as it got in the early days, but the only way to show someone you cared was to come right out and say it. Would we do that now?

Back in wartime, people allowed themselves to be vulnerable because they had no other choice. Not speaking about their feelings or waiting for another moment could mean they never got the chance again. Every second counted. While today we hold our feelings back and don't want to speak out of fear of rejection, back then, the only way to learn whether you had a future with a person was to come right out and tell them.

Everything is heighted when each day could be your last. When you are surrounded by gunfire and violence, you crave the stability and safety of a lover's arms. When the person you love is away fighting on the frontlines, you spend every single day worrying about whether or not you'll ever see their face again, or whether you'll end up burying them as your last lover's duty.

The reality of the situation forced people to speak their hearts. Today, we wait, stumble, and often allow our chances to pass. We take for granted the opportunities we have in front of us and rely too much on technology to do everything for us.

While war raged around the world, humanity could only pull together and fight for the right to freedom and for love. Simply seeing people being human is an act that doesn't tend to come to the fore very often these days. Perhaps it is time to bring the humanity in all of us to be able to truly cherish the freedom and love that our ancestors fought to keep.

The love stories told during World War II were epic because they were uncertain. There were no plans because nobody knew what would happen the next day, let alone the following year. All you could do was dream and hope. Hope that when your lover returned to your arms, you could pick up where you left off and vow never to allow another second to go by without letting them know just what they meant to you.

Do we do that now?

WHAT CAN WE LEARN FROM OUR HEROES & HEROINES?

I hope you have read this book and felt moved with every single story. Now that you have come to know the characters better and felt a tiny amount of their angst and pain, which story is your favorite? Is there one you can identify with more than the others, or do you find yourself drawn to a particular character and their plight?

Ending our series of stories on a tragic tale may seem negative, but it highlights the reality of war all too well. We can focus on the positive stories and find hope amongst the darkness, but the truth is that the majority of lovers never returned. Yet, that doesn't mean the love they experienced was in vain or that it didn't live on in the hearts of those who felt it.

The strength, positivity, focus and faith that every single one of our couples showed is beyond admirable. I personally can't imagine for a second the sheer terror and worry they must have felt, and for those who returned home, the joy they must have experienced when they finally ran into their lover's arms once more. It must have been beyond words.

The majority of our couples have children and grandchildren who allow their love to live on. But what can we learn from their stories?

If reading this book has taught you anything, it's that you should cherish the love you have in your life. You should hold onto it as tight as possible and always speak your mind. If you love your partner, tell them. If they're doing something to annoy you, tell them so you can work it out and focus on making your love deeper!

Communication is something we don't do so well these days, despite the countless new ways to talk to one another. If anything, technology has made us even more tight-lipped because we are all so worried about being pushed away. But if you love someone, of course you should tell them. Even if you've married them and given your vow to stay with them for life – tell them every day how much they mean to you. You never know what day may be your last.

Life is full of ups and downs, and relationships ebb and flow through the years. Every couple has their difficulties, but rather than focusing on the negatives and becoming bogged down by the challenges, why not see them as an opportunity to pull together and grow?

Christopher and Bessie courted through letters – they had no choice but to put their feelings down in words. They didn't let pride get in the way or worry about rejection stopping them from telling each other how they felt.

Felice and Lilly didn't allow prejudices and fear to stop them from cementing their enduring love for one another. Even when it seemed useless, when every hope looked like it was about to be extinguished, they held each other closer and didn't let go until the very last second. Even then, Lilly refused to allow her love for Felice to be tainted or dulled in any way.

People will always have something to say about your life, who you choose to love, what you believe, and what you look like. It's your choice whether you listen to them or your heart. Our couples never allowed the thoughts or prejudices of others to stop them from following their deep love. Ralph and Beryl surely wished they had another day together, or even just a few minutes – but you have that time so don't let it go.

REFERENCES

Aimee & Jaguar. (n.d.). Google Books. https://www.google.com/books/edition/ Aimee_Jaguar/LD1mCwAAQBAJ?hl=en

All for Love. (n.d.). Jewish Museum Berlin. https://www.jmberlin.de/en/all-for-love

Arthur's War. (n.d.). Google Books. https://www.google.com/books/edition/ Arthur_s_War/Xu66cEEGP1cC?hl=en

Beryl Williams and Ralph James. (n.d.). Docest. https://docest.com/beryl-williams-and-ralph-james

Dean, M. (2020, December 16). *World War 2 Letters: Dearest Eleanor*. World War 2 Facts. http://www.worldwar2facts.org/world-war-2-letters-dearest-eleanor.html

Dear Joan. (n.d.). Google Books. https://www.google.com/books/edition/ Dear_Joan/dYWPaqN3O5AC?hl=en

Dearest Letty. (n.d.). Google Books. https://www.google.com/books/edition/ Dearest_Letty/jS5LCgAAQBAJ?hl=en

Felice and Lilly—An Uneasy Berlin Love Story. (2021, March 7). The National WWII Museum | New Orleans. https://www.nationalww2museum.org/war/articles/ felice-and-lilly-uneasy-berlin-love-story

Frumkes, L. S. (n.d.). *Civil Defense Corps*. https://wwiinavydentist.blogspot.com/ 2015/02/civil-defense-corps.html

Letters Live. (2021, April 30). *Benedict Cumberbatch & Louise Brealey read letters from wartime lovers*. YouTube. https://www.youtube.com/watch?v= eeQME5WzTT4

REFERENCES

Love in War: A Review of We Are Going to be Lucky: A World War II Love Story in Letters. (2020, February 3). The National WWII Museum | New Orleans. <span>https://www.nationalww2museum.org/war/articles/love-war-review-we-are-going-be-lucky-world-war-ii-love-story-letters

Love Stephen: A World War II Love Story. (n.d.). Spotify. https://open.spotify.com/show/60UPRAprhN9uo5N51KEy3c

My Dear Bessie. (n.d.). Google Books. https://www.google.com/books/edition/My_Dear_Bessie/JtQ6BAAAQBAJ?hl=en

National Museum of American Jewish Military History. (2019, January 9). *We Are Going to Be Lucky - Elizabeth Fox at the National Museum of American Jewish Military History*. YouTube. https://www.youtube.com/watch?v=wK5WD9aVoKQ

Oregonian, J. W. T. T. (2015, October 2). *NW love stories: Ray and Betty Whipps have been fraternizing for 70 years*. Oregonlive. https://www.oregonlive.com/living/2015/10/nw_love_stories_ray_and_betty.html

Penguin Books Australia. (2010, July 21). *Arthur Bancroft Arthur's War*. YouTube. https://www.youtube.com/watch?v=fdnJ7fWHHjc

'Til We Meet Again. (n.d.). Google Books. https://www.google.com/books/edition/Til_We_Meet_Again/tr_GCQAAQBAJ?hl=en

Tyndale House Publishers. (2015, March 17). *'Til We Meet Again by Ray and Betty Whipps*. YouTube. https://www.youtube.com/watch?v=0MV3e3Oa6bo

We Are Going to Be Lucky. (n.d.). Google Books. https://www.google.com/books/edition/We_Are_Going_to_Be_Lucky/9btdDwAAQBAJ?hl=en

World War II: "Donut Dollies" & the American Red Cross. (2021, April 5). Division of Historical and Cultural Affairs - State of Delaware. https://history.delaware.gov/ww-ii-donut-dollies-the-american-red-cross/

ABOUT THE AUTHOR

Amelia Kenton describes herself as a romance enthusiast. She draws inspiration from the love around her. Her interest in romance made her dig deeper into historical love stories from all across the world. Her intent is to preserve memories and stories of the brave men and women who lived through these tumultuous times.

In her spare time, Amelia and her husband spend time travelling, reading, visiting war memorials and museums as they seem to draw connections to the strength and resilience of the people that existed back then.

Printed in Great Britain
by Amazon

32832911R00066